Also by
MARIE ESTORGE

In the Middle of Otherwise

(penned under Marie Etienne)

Storkbites: A Memoir

Confessions of a Bi-Polar Mardi Gras Queen

D1157649

then there was Larry

a memoir by

marie estorge

Alluvium Books

FIRST EDITION

Designed by David Provolo

Library of Congress Cataloging-in-Publication Data has been applied for.

ISBN 978-0-9748474-4-3

NOTE TO READERS: This is a work of non-fiction. Some names and identifying details have been changed.

For Avery and Burgess

August 21, 2013

WE ALL HAVE SECRETS. In our lives, we've done or heard or thought things that we've chosen not to share with our friends, family, community, and colleagues. Some secrets are as endearing as a caterpillar tickling its way across your toes. Like telling your friend that her baby is adorable despite the newborn's resemblance to E.T. Some secrets are as harmless as a personal pet peeve. Like when your coworker says, "I seen that movie," and you want to grip her by the shoulders and say, "It's 'I *have* seen that movie.'" Some secrets, however, are as poisonous as the Cone Snail with their harpoon-like teeth and paralysis-causing venom—a creature you don't want to brush up against accidentally.

I, like many people, have been stung by creatures who appeared as benign as a caterpillar but were, in fact, more of the Cone Snail variety. And here, my story begins.

At nine PM, highway traffic still strummed outside my bedroom window. Four hours east of my home in Walnut Creek, California, the 2013 Rim Fire was ravaging tens of thousands of acres of forest and displacing hundreds of residents and their pets. Yet, my sons and I and our neighbors were safe. On this particular August night, I was sitting cross-legged in my bed in the company of our two cats, Toby and Shelby, as they spooned on the adjacent pillow. Toby, admittedly my favorite, was the color of our hardwood floors and suffered no petting or attention unless it was at his urging. The little shit loved to bite. He'd saunter over, nudge you to pet him, and then bite your hand when he'd had enough. Conversely, Shelby gave off a vibe of desperation in her attention-seeking, which often guaranteed the opposite outcome. She was sweet, but needy as hell. Her matted black and white furry belly practically dragged on the ground as she wandered from room to room. Even with diet food, she was the size of a bear cub. As much as I wanted to love her equally, her neediness and gluttony annoyed me.

Leaning against the headboard, I peeled off the rubber band on the ever-thinning *Contra Costa Times* and smoothed out the creases in the newspaper. My two college-aged sons, Austin and Zack had left the house after dinner. Backpacks slung over their shoulders. They were driving on one of the winding roads of the San Francisco East Bay hills, looking for vistas and interesting things—abandoned buildings, graffiti, trespassing deer, mirror-like puddles—to photograph. A mug of Earl Grey tea sat on a stack of novels on my nightstand. I skimmed the headlines of the local news and stopped on: *Child porn distributor gets 15 years. Man served three years previously for statutory rape*—sick bastard. I loved reading true crime stories. It amazed me how seemingly ordinary people kept getting caught doing stupid stuff, and often, some pretty disturbing stuff. It especially dumbfounded me how highly-respected people—doctors, professors, actors, clergy, and public officials—would risk their livelihood, their reputation, and their standing in the community by allowing themselves to get caught hooking up with prostitutes, or worse, underage girls or boys. A few years earlier, one of Austin and Zack's favorite middle-school teachers was arrested on molestation charges. As shocked as I was to read about his arrest in the newspaper, I couldn't help thinking back to the school's annual open house where I discovered a comfy sofa in the back of his classroom. A sofa seemed an odd piece of furniture for a classroom. But the teacher was extremely well-liked by faculty, students, and parents, and admittedly, he was pretty attractive. What a disappointment, later, to learn that he'd molested a student during a tutoring session and sent her a bunch of sexual text messages. Still, it baffled me that the family, friends, and colleagues all claimed to have no idea that the accused was such a curb-crawler, or worse, a sociopath. How could you live with someone, sleep under the same high-thread-count sheets and eat at the same dinner table, night after night, and profess your ignorance when it turns out that your husband has been texting dick pics with one of his math students? Weren't there always signs? A sofa in the classroom, for instance. Surely, you would sense something amiss? How could the spouse or partner be so oblivious? It seemed like a matter of not wanting to know. I shook my head in disgust and continued reading.

A Pleasant Hill man was sentenced to 15 years in prison Monday for distributing pornographic videos of young children, sending him back behind bars almost 10 years after he served time for the statutory rape of a 14-year-old girl.

Laurence Pallen, 60 —

What the fuck! Distributing pornography? Statutory rape? That couldn't be the same Larry Pallen I knew. Jane had mentioned that Larry's laptop was confiscated a while back for containing child pornography, which was very shocking, but I thought he'd been released.

I dropped the newspaper and sucked in a deep breath, then shuddered at the faint, yet lingering odor of the previous homeowner's body that was found in what was now our kitchen. When we had toured the home before writing an offer, my son Zack had asked, "What's that smell?" This unpleasant odor and the superstitions attached to deaths had caused the previous buyers to back out of escrow, making it possible for me to keep my sons in our highly rated school district. Despite this smell and the fact that we could see large, reflective highway signs from our bedroom windows—another detail announced by Zack during the tour, the house had air conditioning, a solid roof, and reliable plumbing. And best of all, my friend Winn came over to see our new house and spoke to the spirit of the previous owner. Winn assured me that the woman's spirit said that my sons and I were welcome in her home. This was good news.

I picked up the newspaper and continued reading about the FBI sting named Operation Sunflower. I didn't immediately put the name of the sting together with the flower I had painted on the shed in the back yard. Later, I would think it a strange coincidence.

Laurence Pallen, 60, admitted in his guilty plea April 22 that he used the Internet to share videos of children engaged in sex acts with adults, according to U.S. Attorney . . . Such material was discovered on four different computers, seven external storage drives, and . . .

Holy shit! What a revolting bastard. Toby roused and disengaged himself from Shelby, stretching his long body across the pillow—the pillow that a few years ago Larry's head had rested. Toby head-butted my arm as if to say, "What's up? Why the racing heart? How about scratching my neck?"

"Toby, sweetie," I cooed, pulling him into my lap. "Our dear friend Larry, boring 'ol Larry, well . . . it turns out Larry is a perv. A perv of the worst kind."

Pleasant Hill man . . . served three years previously for statutory rape. This can't be Larry, as in Larry, my ex-boyfriend, I thought. How would I have not known about a previous rape conviction? Could there be two Lawrence Pallens from Pleasant Hill?

I read the article through once, my heart pounding more and more after each sickening detail. I thought about Larry in jail, sleeping in his cold cell, and wanted to chop his dick off. How could he have done such things? My fury and disbelief soon turned to Jane. Surely, she wouldn't have set me up with a rapist! Or did she secretly hate me? Want to humiliate and hurt me? What a bitch. How in the hell would she explain away this one? In my mind, I saw the men and women, former volleyball teammates and friends, who my sons and I had camped out with on the Eel River and spent the 4th of July watching fireworks. Did they think I knew about Larry's past and therefore figured I was either sick or a loser for dating someone so scummy?

Toby nudged my hand with his white-dotted paw. He gave me a look that said, "Gonna scratch my neck or what?" "Not now," I said and set him back on the pillow. I took a sip of my tea that had now turned cold and wondered how I'd missed all the signs. Was I clueless or in denial? Maybe I should have asked more questions.

chapter one

December 31, 2007

MY ON-AGAIN, OFF-AGAIN, close friend Jane unexpectedly called as I was boxing up Christmas ornaments. In her perky, best-pals voice, she said, "I've missed you. We need to catch up. How are you doing?"

"I'm fine," I said. "Diving, writing, playing softball, working, and taking care of the kids. The usual. I'm a little surprised to hear from you."

"Why is that?"

"Well, I kept calling and texting you last summer about the camping trip you invited the boys and me on. You never replied. We even drove to the campsite and couldn't find you."

"Oh, darn. I was having trouble with the kids. You know, it just wasn't a good time."

"So, you didn't end up going."

"Oh, we went. We must have just missed each other. I'm so sorry."

"O-kay," I said sarcastically. I waited to see if my passive-aggressive sarcasm would elicit further apology or explanation, but nothing followed. "So sorry" was the best she could offer.

"Anyway, how are you?" I asked. I figured she was having boyfriend issues and the conversation would quickly pivot to her woes. I was the reliable shoulder to cry on. She was so predictable, and yet, I found her drama pretty entertaining.

"I'm having a New Year's Day party," she said. "You've got to come so I can introduce you to my good friend Larry. I've known him forever. He just broke up with his girlfriend. And, like you, he doesn't drink anymore."

He doesn't drink anymore—a rather flimsy endorsement. Years later, I realized a reasonably curious and cautious single woman might have asked more questions.

Questions I Should Have Asked, #1: Why did they break up?

Questions I Should Have Asked, #2: What caused him to hit bottom and stop drinking? Did she know how often, if ever, he fell off the wagon and what did that look like?

"I'm working tomorrow," I said. "But let's get together next week."

"You're working? Since when? Where?"

"Barnes & Noble. It's just a seasonal job. I figured with my new memoir coming out, it couldn't hurt to make some contacts in the store. Also, they offer a generous employee discount during the holidays."

I tried to sound upbeat about the minimum wage job and the fact that I wasn't really getting the most out of my MBA, but I was ready to turn in my nametag. The holiday rush had been fun, yet exhausting. So, while Jane and her friends were drinking wine, or in Larry's case, club soda, I'd be standing at the register for eight hours trying to sell twenty-five-dollar memberships to hungover bargain shoppers and reciting the store's return policy for those wanting to return their duplicate copies of "Eat, Pray, Love" for post-holiday cash.

"Stop by before work. Larry offered to arrive early to help set up."

Hum. A guy who volunteered to show up early. And help out! After a grueling Christmas Eve shift earlier that week, I'd paid Zack seventy-five dollars for a thirty-minute foot massage, which he couldn't get five dollars on the open market for his lack of enthusiasm and effort.

"Okay. But don't tell Larry that you're trying to set us up. Let's just see if there's any chemistry."

13

After we hung up, I wondered if I should even bother meeting this guy, Larry. Jane's first attempt to set me up had ended badly. She'd brought a former college classmate, recently separated and no kids, to my 40th birthday party in the hopes we'd hit it off, which we did, for a few months. However, accepting a blow job from your soon-to-be-ex-wife wasn't conducive to a budding relationship.

Questions I Should Have Asked, #3: Should I be a little wary of your taste in potential suitors for me?

Then again, I figured, maybe the first setup was an innocent miss. Maybe I should consider it a compliment she'd thought of me, once again, among all her single friends. She obviously thought highly of Larry to recommend him.

If only I'd known how wrong that was.

Her call was, however, timely. I had been thinking about dating, taking that daunting plunge. At work, I'd stand at the register for hours ringing up customers, listening to an endless playlist of holiday songs, while fantasizing about striking up a conversation with a handsome, well-read customer over our favorite books. In my mind, as my fantasy man signed his credit card receipt (no wedding ring, yeah!), he'd say, "I'd love to take you out to dinner to continue this conversation." Soon we'd be a couple. Then the ring, marriage, and happily ever after. It hadn't happened yet, but I was still hopeful.

It had been five years since my last serious boyfriend Mike and I broke up. The biggest hurdle to dating post-divorce had been my sons, Austin and Zack. They didn't like the first man I dated after their father, and they both, to different degrees, disliked and distrusted Mike. He reneged on a promise to pay Austin—eleven years old and immensely shy at the time—twenty-five dollars if he spoke on his behalf at a packed city council meeting. On a school night, no less. Then there was the time he hired his own young sons and mine to pull weeds on a steep and prickly hillside one scorching August weekend, and when the exhausted, sunburnt boys quit after the first full day, he refused to prorate their pay—insisting it was an all-or-nothing job. *Fucker.* And god forbid he catch me negotiating with Zack, "Come on, one bite of salmon and then you can have as much spätzle and broccoli as you want." Suddenly, I was the worst, most indulgent mom in the world. Yeah, it took a while, but I finally got it. There was no room in our lives for major league assholes.

So, five years later, when Jane invited me over to meet her long-time friend Larry, I was ready to date again, trusting that not all men were double-crossing control-freaks. Plus, Austin and Zack were in high school and more independent. We'd done a lot of individual and family therapy. Just because they hadn't liked or trusted Mike didn't mean they'd dislike or distrust my next boyfriend. I simply needed to make better choices.

New Year's Day morning, I soaked in the tub, sipping tea and mentally preparing myself to meet Larry. This could be my re-entry into the dating world, I thought, giddy with both excitement and fear. I looked down at the half-submerged topography of my naked body and tried to see it from a man's point of view, as if he were visiting the terrain for the first time. The smooth plains of my youth had given way to the rolling hills of middle age. Forty-five years of wear and tear. Silvery stretch marks snaked slyly up and over the hillsides, abruptly halting at a C-section scar running horizontally through my pubic region. My legs, luckily, were still strong and firm from diving, hiking, and softball. I hadn't wrinkled around the eyes and mouth as much as some of my friends. My brown hair was quickly turning a silky, silvery blond, and springboard diving afforded me a year-round tan. A shallow man might take a quick glance, see a middle-aged single mom who's not especially skinny and lose interest, but surely a guy with any discernment would see how awesome I am. I hoped.

And hopefully, Larry was one of those discerning and rare men who believed that it's what is inside that counts the most. Looking at myself from this angle, how marketable was I as a girlfriend or lover? There was the mental illness—bipolar and depression. Pre-diabetes. Financial worries. My occasional scary temper.

Despite these issues, maybe it isn't too late for me, I thought. I had a lot to offer. I was not a bad catch. It was the sum of the parts, not the individual parts themselves, that mattered. I had a lot of friends. People were always laughing at my one-liners or asides. My handmade purses and sculptures, as well as my published essays and memoir, drew a lot of compliments. I was known for my generosity, kindness, and honesty. I could whip up yummy sweets from my childhood: pecan pies, pralines, carrot cakes. I could, on a good day, hit a softball into left field for a double or chuck a back one-and-a-half somersault with a half-twist on a three-meter springboard. I threw fun parties and had lots of hobbies (golf and tennis in addition to softball and diving) and interests (writing, reading, traveling, and movies). Maybe Larry, or some other man, would be excited to date me.

But then, there was the fact I'd spent a lot of money on self-publishing my first, and soon my second memoir and on expensive family vacations. I'd received the second half of a million-dollar inheritance, and less than a year later, with two teenage sons to support and a huge mortgage, and no proper paying job in years, I'd blown through most of my stocks and bonds. Money was a constant worry. Of my six siblings, I was nearly broke. I was the one whose son asked, "Mom, how'd we get to be so poor?"

List these good and bad attributes—physical and otherwise—on a resume, and I knew I wouldn't be anyone's first draft pick. More than likely, a third or fourth-round pick unless the suitor was a similarly a mixed bag of goods. As it turned out, someone like Larry.

chapter two

I SLIPPED ON MY most slimming black slacks and sweater, applied makeup (a rarity), blow-dried my hair (even rarer), and practiced smiling and saying hello in the bathroom mirror, approving of my just-bleached teeth. Beauty tip: always restock your professional-grade bleach during a bi-annual dental visit.

"Happy New Year!" I said. Jane and I hugged and kissed at her front door of her rancher. I held out a bottle of Mums and she took my hand, leading me through the living room decorated with her teenage daughter's impressive artwork and past the dining room table set with flowers and candles. The music wasn't yet playing, but there would be music. Jane loved to dance. Hand-in-hand like schoolgirls, we entered the kitchen to find Larry standing over a cutting board and smashing a head of garlic with his palm. As promised, he had arrived early to help prepare. I watched him skillfully peel away the sticky skin from a clove and thought, *Impressive.* His hands were nice for someone who worked with tools all day. Nails clean, unbitten.

"Larry," she said in a sing-song voice. "This is my dear friend Marie. A published author, an excellent cook, springboard diver, and mom to two adorable boys." He turned and wiped his hands on a dishtowel. His thin lips formed into a polite, if not somewhat strained, smile. He leaned against the counter as if bracing himself. A slight belly protruded over the belt of his jeans. I sucked in my stomach and smiled confidently.

"Marie, this is Larry," Jane continued, as he stood quietly, giving no hint of his initial assessment. "He's been helping me with some handyman projects around my house. We've known each other since our early volleyball days, when the kids were all running around in diapers. Larry even coached for quite a while."

Questions I Should Have Asked, #4: Why did he stop coaching?

We shook hands. Larry glanced at Jane's cleavage. Red patches of spider veins decorated his nose and cheeks, presumably a result of a heyday of drinking and repeated overexposure to the sun from his handyman work and coaching.

"It's a pleasure to meet you." His eyes darted from me back to the plunging neckline of Jane's sundress. Her high, round breasts were quite impressive. Obviously, Larry was finding it extremely difficult to ignore the view as Jane shared an anecdote about how I was afraid of heights (not true) but forced myself to jump and later flip off the three-meter diving board at the swim school where I practiced. She spoke about my determination and praised my writing, although I don't think she'd ever read more than a few paragraphs of what I'd written or published. Still, I was flattered by the enthusiastic endorsement.

Throughout our conversation, I kept checking Jane's expression for a sign that she'd noticed Larry's ogling and was getting annoyed. He wasn't, after all, a thirteen-year-old who'd just discovered that Mrs. Cleaver had hooters. She carried on as if unaware. Knowing Jane, as I thought I did, I figured she wasn't too polite or shy to say, "Uh, Larry, my eyes are up here." Rather, she seemed to enjoy the attention and became increasingly animated and wiggly in her sundress.

"So, you're a writer," he said, briefly making eye contact. "What are you working on?"

I was grateful he didn't say something dismissive like, "That's a nice hobby." I gave him a quick synopsis of the novel and described an intentionally disastrous yet hopefully funny sex scene I'd just finished writing before heading to Jane's house.

Jane laughed along with Larry. "You probably didn't expect to hear *that* coming from this sweet, soft-spoken southern lady."

He shook his head and finally peeled his eyes off of her cleavage. I'd grabbed his attention. Amazing how sex will do that! I regaled them with another anecdote. It was fun seeing the surprise on Larry's face.

I asked if he was much of a reader, and he named a couple of authors, whom I didn't recognize besides James Patterson. I figured they wrote crime novels or thrillers, genres that held little interest for me. But still . . . he liked to read! And apparently, he enjoyed sports, or at least, he did at one time. Maybe with a little push, he'd be back out on a volleyball court. I loved to play volleyball, but I'd little opportunity to do so, other than Club Med and the all-inclusive vacations my sons and I took. The few times I'd joined drop-in games in my area, the players were so competitive and unwelcoming. The conversation moved on to kids. I asked if he had any children and his face lit up. He told me he had a son who was finishing college out-of-state. They were extremely close, he said. I liked that he seemed so proud of him.

After a few minutes, the effort to be funny and interesting and curious exhausted me.

"It's been really nice meeting you," I said to Larry. "I've got to run. Work calls." This was the awkward part where the girl hoped and waited for the guy to say, "I'd love to call you sometime. Give me your number?" Larry smiled. I waited. His attention diverted back to Jane's cleavage. Nervously, I made a preemptive strike, saying, "If you'd like to walk the Lafayette Reservoir or have coffee sometime, you can get my contact information from Jane."

As I headed to my car, I wondered what answers Larry was giving to Jane's grilling: "So what do you think? Are you interested? Do you find her attractive?" When she grilled me later, what feedback would I share?

The excitement and speculation of where things with Larry might go fizzled out by the time I pulled into the parking lot of Barnes & Noble. My eagerness turned to fear: what if he turns out to be an asshole like the last guy Jane set me up with? Then practicality: If he's not the one, then at least I'd opened the door for more promising prospects. It was time to get serious about finding a boyfriend. The longer I sat on the market like a mid-century property, the longer I deferred maintenance and let time and weather take their toll, the less demand I would attract from qualified, eager buyers. Fear whispered in my ear: if things aren't great now, what might they be in another year, another decade?

Please call, I prayed as I headed to the elevator. Even though I couldn't claim he had set off any majestic sparks, he seemed nice enough. It couldn't hurt to invest some time in getting to know him.

chapter three

JANE AND I had lunch shortly after New Year's Day. She said Larry thought I was pretty and nice. He said he planned to call me. She was surprised he hadn't yet, but told me to be patient.

A couple of weeks passed and Larry still hadn't called. I figured he wasn't interested and had perhaps told Jane that he'd had a change of heart. I was too embarrassed to ask her. But the rejection stung. I hadn't even been given a real chance. I was indignant, wondering if he thought *he* could do better than me. I had an MBA, my writing, two adorable sons, hobbies, an accounting career I could fall back, and a lot of friends and family who seemed to genuinely care about me. I definitely had my shortcoming as dating material, but it wasn't as if he were the world's greatest catch. In fact, he ticked off a few boxes that might cause a lot of women to dismiss him without a second glance. He was an alcoholic handyman—so rule out any gold-diggers, which I wasn't. He was somewhat attractive and still had a decent head of salt and pepper hair, but in all honesty, what was with the crusty teeth? Could he not afford a cleaning? Then, there were the spider veins and Rosacea. I wasn't usually one to judge someone on looks entirely, but if I needed to find faults, I could. Plus, I couldn't recall anything really interesting he talked about other than he used to play and coach volleyball and had a son whom he adored.

Surely, he could see that it was he who was lucky that I'd proposed a walk or coffee. He'd be dating up, not down. These thoughts helped prop up my self-esteem for a few days, but then I started the familiar mind-talk: Had I come off as too forward or desperate in asking him out first? Had he read my first memoir, *Storkbites*, and decided that I had too much personal baggage? If this Average Joe didn't want me, what chances did I have that someone better would want me?

As the days passed, I considered driving by Jane's house, and if I spotted Larry's old dented truck in the driveway, knocking at her door and pretending I was simply in the neighborhood. Each time, I nixed this idea because I didn't want to find her and Larry standing in her front yard, talking while she hand watered her flowers and plants, then look up to see me driving past. That would be humiliating. I considered calling her under some other pretense and casually asking if Larry was still doing handyman work around her house. How was it going with his ex-girlfriend? Had they gotten back together? I wondered if she'd act surprised that he hadn't yet called or would drop the news that he wasn't interested, after all. Another potentially awkward situation.

In early February, Larry finally called and asked if I'd like to meet at the Lafayette Reservoir. Despite my annoyance at his waiting over a month to call, I considered his suggestion for a hike to be a positive sign—he was willing to commit to more than a quick cup of coffee. If he turned out to be a bore or was, in fact, disinterested in me and had called only out of loyalty to Jane, at least it was a beautiful February day for exercising and people watching. And if by some lark it went well, I would suggest we go for coffee or lunch.

Before climbing out of the car in the parking lot, I applied a fresh coat of red lipstick, checked my nose for flakes and teeth for food particles, and fluffed out my hair. Waiting next to the water fountain and communal dog bowl, Larry shuffled from foot to foot. *That's cute,* I thought. *He looks nervous.* From a distance, he was a fairly attractive man. I hoped he thought the same of me. I gave a brief wave as I approached.

"It's nice to see you," I said. His hands stuffed in his pockets spared me the awkward decision of whether to shake hands or hug.

"You too." He smiled, revealing his less than sparkly teeth.

"Do you have a preference?" I asked. "Upper or lower trail?" *Please say lower.* On my last hike with Jane, she'd proposed the upper dirt trail and even though I was reasonably active, I had to stop every twenty yards to catch my breath. By the time I got back to my car, my face was as red as a pomegranate.

He pointed to the lower asphalt trail and said, "This is fine with me." *Thank you, dear Jesus!* "I'm having some trouble with my ankles." *That's not good.* I definitely wanted someone who was active and structurally sound.

Immediately, I launched into an easy line of questioning as I'm inclined to do when nervous and wanting to divert attention away from me: "How's your weekend going? Are you originally from California? Are your parents still alive? Siblings?" I was trying to avoid the pressing questions: "So why did it take you so long to call me? Are you still dating that other woman? Do you ever fall off the wagon? When was the last time you flossed your teeth?"

His answers were brief. He had two brothers. He got along with his ex-wife and her family. *Good signs.* He was a handyman. He rented a room in Oakland from one of his friends. His answers revealed nothing unexpected. Either he was nervous or simply going through the motions.

"Do you like going to the movies?" I asked after a few quiet minutes. When he said yes, I listed my recent favorite rom-coms and dramas and asked about his. It turned out he wasn't as avid a movie-goer as I was. We moved on to books, travel, fun anecdotes about our children. He asked how my writing was going. I loved it when people asked about my writing. It made my work and ambition feel legitimate. Not some frivolous waste of time and money.

"Are you still working on Jane's house?" I asked.

"Done for now. I'm working on the gay bathroom this week?" He chuckled.

"Gay bathroom?" I pictured a steamy, communal gay bathhouse in San Francisco with beautifully ornate tile. *You go, Larry! So maybe you're not so boring.*

"Yeah. A friend whom Jane and I have known for decades decided last year that he's gay. Jumped the fence, you know. I'm redoing his bathroom. I call it the Gay Bathroom."

"That name doesn't offend him?"

"Naw. I don't think so."

The conversation stalled again. The only follow-up I could think of was: *You live in California, for Christ's sake. What kind of person talks like that anymore?* So far, Larry didn't appear to be very promising, long-term dating material. He could turn into a casual friend to see the occasional movie or have lunch, but I couldn't imagine us becoming serious. Maybe being single parents and non-drinkers weren't enough to base a relationship on.

"So, you've known Jane a few years?" he asked after another awkward silence.

"My older son Austin started in the same preschool class as her son Josh. Later, they played soccer together and I led their Cub Scout den. While our sons chased soccer balls and explored the inner workings of the Caldecott Tunnel, Jane and I fell into a fast, easy friendship where we exchanged divorce stories and talked about the challenges of dating when you have young children."

Larry nodded. He touched my arm and motioned for me to move aside to let a trio of joggers pass. I watched the college-aged girls' Lycra-clad butts as they jogged around us, their ponytails swinging back and forth, and I wished I still looked that firm and round from behind. From the way his eyes followed their asses, apparently, Larry was enjoying the view.

We stopped at the first water fountain and I gulped down tepid but satisfying mouthfuls. We hadn't even reached the halfway mark of our walk and already, my lungs were burning. I breathed deeply, the scent of the nearby tall Eucalyptus trees.

"And damn, Josh is smart." I wiped a drop of water off my chin with the back of my hand. "Funny as well. I drove him and Austin to school a few times, and unlike Austin—who volunteers nothing to other adults—Josh was a total chatterbox. And not the annoying stuff that know-it-all kids spew, but interesting observations and questions."

"He's a sweet kid," Larry said. "And active. There were a handful of times when he was younger that Jane would call and say, 'Can you just take him off my hands for a few hours?'"

"Really?" Unlike me, Jane always seemed to have an unlimited supply of patience. As an often-insecure parent, I secretly envied her insistence and unequivocal belief that she was an excellent, superior parent. One minute she'd be apologizing to a soccer parent for her son's misdeed, and the next, she'd be doling out unsolicited advice to the same unreceptive, pissed off parent. Her audacious gift for turning the situation back on the other party always entertained me.

"Look at that couple," I said. An elderly couple was walking ahead of us and holding hands. "They're out here at least two or three days a week. My friend Lynne and I always see them." Larry said hello to the couple as we overtook them and walked ahead. "I've never heard them speak to each other," I whispered after some distance. "But they look so content."

"Are you still working at the book store?" he asked.

"No, it was just a holiday gig. Has Jane ever told you how she applied for a job at Barnes & Noble in college?"

Larry shook his head.

"The manager kept turning her down, explaining that they weren't hiring. But she showed up every day and sat outside the store until he finally gave her a job. I love that she's so outspoken and persistent. I need her kind of determination."

"She definitely knows what she wants."

"Have you always been a handyman?" I really wanted to ask if he'd been to college, but I didn't want to embarrass him if he hadn't—which I suspected was the case.

"No. I worked for Home Depot for a while," he said, and scratched behind his ear.

Questions I Should Have Asked, #5: Why did you leave Home Depot?

"Before that, I did some union work. But I like the freedom of being my own boss. I do a lot of work for my friends and ex-in-laws. They've always got something for me to do when the funds get low."

There wasn't a hint of shame in sharing this fact. Was Larry his friends and ex-in-laws' charity case? Who knew, maybe one day I'd be hitting up my friends for work. I knew that people, myself included, fell on hard times. It was a tough economy. President Bush's six-hundred-dollar Stimulus Rebate Checks wouldn't do much to change the lives or fortunes of the millions of unemployed. Even though I was nervous about my own finances, I always figured I had enough to share. Certainly, Larry's friends and family would not want to see him struggle.

"That's nice of them," I said. "I'll often find odd jobs around my house for friends who are going through a rough patch financially. I've hired moms and dads from my sons' school or my softball group to paint my house, refinish my hardwood floors, prune my roses, do my holiday shopping, or hang drywall. Some of the kids from my dive club have helped me with my publishing business. One time, when

I couldn't think of any other projects, I paid my friend's girlfriend twenty dollars an hour to organize my shoes and magazines."

We slowed down to watch a deer eating foliage at the edge of the path. The recent rain had caused some minor mudslides. There was rustling farther up the hillside where two deer waited. They were such pretty, timid creatures. In the animal kingdom, I'd definitely be the deer, and Jane, the bear.

"Did you know that Jane restored and flipped motorcycles in high school to earn money for college?" I asked. Larry shook his head. "It's weird how some people's brains are wired just to know how to do something. The closest skill I have to hers is duplicating a dish without the recipe. I guess I've also figured out how to build a website. Are you good with computers?"

Larry shrugged. "I can do what I need to do on them."

Questions I Should Have Asked, #6: Exactly what is it you need to do on them?

For the next quarter-mile, we walked in silence. When we reached the end of our loop around the reservoir, we stopped for water at the fountain next to the children's play area. I watched a German Shepherd loudly lap up water from the community dog bowl while Larry glanced over at the young kids climbing and running around the play structure.

Just as we were about to say goodbye in the parking lot, he said, "I didn't call you until now because I'm sure Jane mentioned that I had been dating someone. I wanted to make sure that was all wrapped up before I asked you out. But now that's done."

"She mentioned a recent ex-girlfriend. Are you okay about it ending?"

"Oh, yeah." He sucked in a deep breath. "She was a terrible alcoholic. The mean kind. You know?"

Yes, I did. I smiled at him. His observation about his alcoholic ex-girlfriend was the wittiest, most interesting thing he'd said since our walk began. "Well," I said, "call me if you want to walk again or have lunch. Or maybe see a movie."

I held my hand out to shake his. He seemed surprised that I'd suggested a second date. Rather than shake my hand, he moved closer and clumsily hugged me.

"I need to make some progress on the Gay Bathroom," he said. *Enough with the homophobic language.* "Then I should have more time."

I smiled but felt as if I had just gotten a polite brush-off. *Well, I tried.*

chapter four

A WEEK AFTER our get-to-know-you walk, Larry called and invited me to dinner. My sons were with their father and Fridays were typically my movie night with friends, but I figured, sure, why not? Maybe he had been nervous, tongue-tied on our walk. Maybe hidden below his dull exterior lies something intriguing and exciting. Anything was possible, right. As for his homophobic sense of humor, perhaps some education could eradicate that foolishness. If nothing else, the evening would be good dating practice.

Larry insisted I choose the restaurant. It wasn't clear if he was trying to be polite and accommodating, or if he was avoiding the pressure of making the first big decision, or if he simply lacked imagination and initiative. I suspected it was a blend of the four. His vibe suggested nothing adventurous, so my favorite Ethiopian place in Berkeley was out. I picked a reasonably priced Thai place in downtown Walnut Creek.

Over spring rolls and Thai iced tea, he updated me on the Gay Bathroom. I tried to feign interest as he explained every nitty-gritty detail of the remodel project—from toilet to vanity to tile.

"So, your friend really doesn't mind you calling it a gay bathroom?" I asked.

"I don't really call it that in front of him."

"Makes sense." Then why say it at all, I wondered, if he knew it was offensive? He shared the backstory of his friendship with the guy. For years they'd played volleyball and enjoyed dozens of mutual friends. The guy had been an unapologetic womanizer. Now he sported an earring and visited gay bars as if the former made the latter a given. I told him about three guys I'd dated and had the biggest crushes on who were now gay. One former lover (and still a dear friend) told me over dinner, years after we'd stopped dating, that he'd *expanded* his dating to include men and how it took me a few seconds to understand what he meant.

"I called my younger sister each time one of these guys came out to me, and she laughed. 'Duh, Marie. You're just figuring that out.'"

Larry smiled and fiddled with his egg roll.

"I mean, I've always been pretty open-minded. So, at first, I didn't understand why they didn't say something years earlier. But then again, I learned, it wasn't always easy for them. Family and friends weren't always so accepting. Maybe they thought I'd shun them as well." Larry nodded and changed the subject to the new red truck that Jane had just purchased for him.

"I've never seen someone just whip out a personal check as if it's no big deal." He shook his head. His astonishment was cute. "Of course, I'm going to get a loan so I can pay her back." He reached for the bill and said, "Jane and I are talking about flipping houses together."

"That's great. Do you want help with the check?"

"Nah. The Gay Bath is paying for dinner."

Inwardly, I cringed. I had my work cut out for me to make him presentable to my friends. On the plus side, however, he was paying for dinner, a rarity. I missed men opening doors, standing when a woman left the table, and paying for meals without calculating who owes what down to the penny.

While we waited for the server to return with his credit card, Larry explained how Jane would put up all the money for their first foreclosed property and he'd earn sweat equity.

marie estorge

"Great for you guys. Sucks for the displaced homeowner." Not wanting to be a killjoy, I said, "I've always wanted to flip houses. I've redone almost every room in my house and have a dozen more projects in mind when, and if, I win the lottery." For a moment, I hoped he'd suggest that I ask Jane about coming on board with the flip. Instead, he said, "Ready?" and pushed back from the table.

He dropped me off in my driveway. I hopped out quickly to avoid figuring out if we should hug or kiss at the door.

"Next time, dinner is on me," I said before closing the truck door.

I set my purse down on the dining room table and smiled. The date hadn't been horrible. He was nice. He wasn't the most exciting or mysterious man I'd ever met, but maybe it wouldn't hurt to heed my older sister's advice—avoid the bad boys and drama, find someone nice and dependable.

Over the next few days, I focused on my sons and my writing. By Wednesday, I wondered if he'd call about the upcoming weekend. It appeared he wasn't one of those needy, over-zealous guys who glommed onto you after the first date. That was good, I supposed. Finally, Thursday afternoon, he phoned to see if I was available on Friday. "Cutting it close, aren't you," I wanted to say.

Once again, it wasn't a killer date. He didn't surprise me with a visit to an art gallery or a picnic in the Mt. Diablo open space. There were no flowers or chocolates or compliments. If a great date was bananas flambé, this date was more a scoop of vanilla ice cream. After dinner, he set the truck in park in my driveway, left the engine running, and walked me to the door. We hugged goodnight.

The next week, he called to chat a few times. On Friday, after a movie and dinner, he gave me a brief kiss at the door, then stuffed his hands into his jean pockets. "I had fun tonight. I'll call you after Las Vegas," he said. He was celebrating his fifty-something birthday in Las Vegas with some of his volleyball buddies whom, except for Jane,

I hadn't yet met but had heard many camping stories about. The fact that he had male friends and they went on adventures that required a boarding pass made Larry seem incredibly more interesting. I could also imagine a half dozen middle-aged men, playing slot machines, and visiting one buffet after another with naps in between.

"Have fun and don't get into too much trouble," I said. Although, I really hoped he would return with some fun, crazy tales to share with Jane and me. Exciting stories that fell somewhere between seeing Liberace's piano to waking up with a tiger in his hotel room. The realization that I was growing fond of him surprised me. Career-wise, he'd never be accused of being overly ambitious. He didn't give me yummy butterflies. But he never suggested I style my hair differently, or wear contacts and change my wardrobe, or lose weight. He seemed to like me well enough, just as I was. There wasn't some better version of Marie he was pressing me for. As long as I wasn't expecting Brad Pitt or Michael Douglas, he had some potential as a boyfriend.

When he returned from his birthday weekend, we went out again and this time, I asked if he wanted to turn off his truck and come in for tea. I set two mugs of chamomile tea on the coffee table and we sat on the sofa, each on our own cushion. This had to be the most awkward part of dating sober. How do you go from sipping tea and discussing an article you read in the newspaper to leaning in for a kiss? What more could we say about the movie we hadn't already?

"Want to play scrabble?" I asked and then hesitated. *What if he can't spell?* I didn't want to embarrass him. He hadn't attended more than a semester or two of college and didn't have an extensive vocabulary. Still, he said he liked to read. We set up the board between us on the sofa and selected our tiles.

As he contemplated his first move, I said, "We don't have to keep score." He shrugged and laid down a word. I don't recall the word he played only that I was impressed enough to feel like a snob for assuming he was only semiliterate and a hypocrite given that I had taken remedial English my freshman year of college. Once we ran out of tiles and played what remaining letters we could, I cleared the board and set the box on the table. Knees to knees, we sat there awkwardly.

"Well, I should go." He yawned, and I caught a whiff of his breath. At what point in our relationship, I wondered, could I introduce him to my dentist? "I've got to get up early tomorrow."

"All right," I said, disappointed. I'd hoped we'd kiss for a while and maybe he'd even stay over. Now that the idea of having sex again in my lifetime didn't seem so remote, I was eager to move things along. We kissed briefly at the door and then hugged goodnight. In retrospect, his lack of desire or disinterest was a clear signal that something was amiss.

chapter five

THE GAY BATHROOM was completed. Jane and his ex-wife's family and other friends continued to find or create jobs for Larry because, I assumed, he earned just enough money to cover his rent, truck upkeep, food, cell phone, and minimum credit card payments. Because of pre-existing condition (thyroid cancer) and being self-employed, he had no health insurance. No savings. No property except for interest in the house his ex-wife lived in and a small union pension coming later. On paper, especially in California, he was basically poor. In an unspoken agreement, I began paying for our meals. On the rare occasion he offered to pay for dinner, it was usually pizza or burritos, and then I'd reciprocate by buying the movie, popcorn, and soda. I still hadn't introduced him to my sons, but he had met my softball friends, including Lynne—who agreed with the others that Larry was nothing like Mike; he was very *nice*, less dashing, but also less narcissistic. We had lunch or dinner with Jane more often as her newest relationship spiraled toward death.

Our courtship chugged along. We finally added some heavy kissing and petting on the sofa to our after-movie routine. And then, for several weeks, things stalled again. We hadn't yet made that short trek from the living room down the hallway to my bedroom. Each time, just before the first button or zipper was breached, he'd pull away, adjust his jeans, and as he rushed out the door, leaving me frustrated and baffled, he'd tell me I got him so excited and that if he weren't a gentleman, he'd devour me. For weeks, he'd say, as he hurried to his truck, that it took a world of restraint not to give in to the desire he felt for me.

Questions I Should Have Asked, #7: Why do you feel a need to restrain yourself? Aren't we both consenting adults?

We only necked on the sofa when my sons were at their dad's house. It wasn't as if I was expecting us to have mad sex on the dining room table while the kids played Legos in the next room. If it were diseases he worried about, I was happy to provide a clean bill of health.

Questions I Should Have Asked, #8: Are you delaying further intimacy because you've got something you don't want to disclose?

If he was concerned about revealing something embarrassing, I thought, it was time for him to strap on his big boy pants and be forthright with me. If I hadn't been so insecure about my desirability, I might have listened to the little voice that kept whispering something was not right here. Instead, I convinced myself we were taking it slow. Really frustratingly slow. Slow was good. After all, I didn't want to be hurt again as I had been with Mike.

In addition to Fridays, we began meeting for coffee at Starbucks in Moraga after I dropped my sons off at school. We'd sit at a table and hold hands like high schoolers. He'd tell me in great detail what had happened on the latest episode of *House*, one of the regular television shows he watched. My sons and I had a no-TV policy during the school week. I had no reference or interest in the characters or plots he'd described, but I'd feign interest. When it was my turn, I'd share something funny the boys said during the morning drive. Or recap an interesting article or column I'd read in the newspaper the night before. We'd laugh over the latest dating advice doled out by Amy Alkon, the witty, no-holds-barred Advice Goddess whose syndicated column I read devotedly. Larry would always act interested. Was it genuine, or was he humoring me as well? It was difficult to say.

Honestly, I never probed too deeply into his thoughts. Our relationship wasn't developing into one of those relationships where all we talked about was *us*. I wasn't one of those partners who constantly asked, "What are you thinking?" We had a nice, uncomplicated, somewhat boring, and perhaps superficial relationship. He let me pick the movies and he didn't complain or nod off, snoring loudly if one of them was terrible.

A couple of months into our dating, I invited Larry to dinner to meet my sons. The evening was a test. I wanted to get a sense of whether he'd hit it off with Austin and Zack: would they tolerate him, and would he tolerate my tendency to overindulge them? Before he arrived, I told them that Larry and I had recently begun dating. I said that he was a nice guy and we often saw movies while they were at their dad's house.

At dinner, I was relieved that Larry didn't act like their new best pal, and later when we played pickleball in the driveway, he didn't need to prove himself as the big man and win every point. He kept a respectable distance from me, no stolen kisses or handholding. He didn't insist on a response if his inquiries to the boys went unanswered. I'd prepped him by saying the boys were shy in front of adults. He accepted this and didn't seem to take it as a sign of disrespect, as Mike and other adults sometimes did. When he launched into a very overly detailed account of his handyman workday, my sons listened attentively rather than fidgeting or asking to play Nintendo games. I figured his familiar anecdotes were new and interesting to them. Fortunately, he'd long since completed the Gay Bathroom job, so he didn't say anything derogatory or homophobic. I didn't want them to think that mom's boyfriend was tactless and mean.

We were finishing our turkey tacos when Larry mentioned that he had hundreds of albums stored in his roommate's garage. "Would you like to see my collection," he asked my sons. "Maybe pick out a few albums for yourselves. I might have an extra turntable and some speakers?"

Their blues eyes grew wide with excitement. Larry smiled. I was relieved that his offer didn't sound creepy, like some stranger in a windowless white van. A few years earlier, there was a middle-aged employee who worked at a pottery studio in Walnut Creek where I'd taken the boys several times to paint clay pieces. This man, demonstrably gay, asked my sons if they wanted to go into the back of the store to see the kiln where they fired the pieces. "We'd love to," I said, as my sons shyly nodded and started to follow him. I knew then, and now, that being gay doesn't make a person a pedophile, but I had an uneasy feeling about how intently the man looked at my sons' faces. When we reached the door to the employee-only section of the studio, he said, "Mom, you can wait here. We'll be right back."

"Thanks, but I'll come along," I said. "I'd love to see the kiln." That incident popped into my head now, as it did from time to time. All modestly aside, but my sons were beautiful children with their big blue eyes and blonde hair. In public, they'd often ask why an adult was staring at them. The attention made them uncomfortable. Sometimes, the attention was due to their acting up, but usually, it seemed just an invasive fascination. Luckily, Larry wasn't some stranger giving off icky vibes. Regardless, I would be there in the garage to make sure nothing weird or inappropriate happened.

Austin asked Larry which albums he had in his collection. His father's love of music had rubbed off on him and Zack.

"That's a really nice offer," I said. "Are you sure you want to give away some of your albums?"

"Yeah. They're just collecting dust. Maybe this weekend after they're back from their dad's house?"

A few days later, after the successful dinner, I'd arrived at Starbucks for our morning meetup prepared. I'd come to a decision. If there were some reason—physical or otherwise—for Larry's reluctance to become physically intimate, I wanted to know sooner rather than later, before either of us invested more time and before my kids became attached to him. If, say, he had a dick the size of a pinkie, I wanted to know so I could decide whether to go or to stay. If he had some dysfunction that a little blue pill couldn't alleviate, I wanted to know so I could decide whether to go or to stay. If he had every STD known to humankind, I wanted to know so I could decide whether to go or to stay. Whatever it was, and my imagination was dancing, I wanted to know while it was still early enough to walk away with no hard feelings.

"You know what today is?" I said, as we held hands across the table. He shook his head. His green eyes really were his best feature. "Our twelfth date," I whispered so that the nearby tables of moms, dads, and St. Mary's students wouldn't overhear us.

His Adam's apple froze mid-swallow. He asked, "Already?"

"Yep. Don't you think it's time we consummate this relationship?"

"Sure. Yeah. Of course."

I wished later that I'd taken a mental snapshot of his face when I set out my proposal. *Was there some flicker, some hint of terror or disappointment racing behind those green eyes? Was there a look of dread I missed?*

"I thought we were just waiting for the right time." He let go of my hand to pick his thumbnail, as he often did when nervous. "But I'm ready if you are."

Questions I Should Have Asked, #9: Why are you so nervous? What is it you're afraid of?

Coincidentally, Larry had mentioned that Jane's soon to be ex-boyfriend hired him to do some repairs on his mother's house in Paso Robles, four hours south of Walnut Creek. Now, he suggested I come along. I could shop in town on Saturday while he worked on the repairs, then we'd have the evenings to ourselves. I felt the swell of relief. We had a plan. There really wasn't anything strange going on here: no physical issue or dysfunction that he was hiding; it was simply a matter of timing.

On Thursday, the day before we were to leave, we met for coffee.

"So, bad news," he said, picking his nail again. "The job in Paso Robles has been delayed for a week, perhaps more. I'm really disappointed," he added, his eyes lowered as he rotated his coffee cup half a turn. "I was looking forward to being alone with you."

Okay, I thought. *This makes no sense. The last nine or ten times we were alone, there was nothing preventing us from having wild sex on every surface in my house if that's what we decided to do. And he surely couldn't use my sons as an excuse since they were at their dad's house three out of every four weekends of the month.*

"I've got a suggestion," I said. I wasn't going to let what little momentum we'd built slide off a cliff if I could help it. Lowering my voice, I said, "Let's book a hotel in San Francisco for Saturday." I glanced around to see if any of the regular Starbucks crowd were looking our way. "My sons will be with their dad. The cats, obviously, can look after themselves for a day."

He kept fidgeting with his coffee cup, but I managed to loosen a smile.

"Let's book a room at the Sir Francis Hotel. We'll spend the afternoon looking at galleries and then go out for a nice dinner. And last, but not least, we can christen our relationship in luxurious linen sheets."

His silence and nervousness were disheartening. *What is your problem?* Either he was too embarrassed to admit he couldn't afford a nice hotel room or an expensive dinner in the city, or there was truly a reason he was avoiding intimacy with me. *Whatever it was, time's up, fella!* To thwart any attempt to weasel his way out, I added, "My treat. I'll pay for everything."

Once he'd agreed, I thought, *next . . . the really difficult part.* A few minutes later, we stood in the parking lot, leaning against my car and holding hands. Nervously, I said, "I've got something to tell you." It was never clear when was the right time to disclose to friends and colleagues my diagnosis. "I'm bipolar." His face remained impassive. "I manage it very well with medicine. I've got that plus intermittent depression." He held my hands but still said nothing. "Have I scared you off?" I asked, looking for clues in his green eyes. To my relief, he finally chuckled and then hugged me.

He said, in his Larry-like way, "That's okay. My last girlfriend, as you know, was a terrible alcoholic."

I felt such relief. When I'd told Mike about the diagnosis, after we'd broken up but still talked daily (we were going to try to remain close friends despite the fact he was *finding* himself by screwing his way through Contra Costa County), he recoiled. He looked at me as if I'd just told him I'd been diagnosed with leprosy. Just one sneeze from too narrow a distance, and bam, I'd infect him with a disease that might interfere with his busy softball schedule.

"Do you have any disclosures?" I asked. "Any dark secrets or STDs you need to disclose?"

He squeezed my hands and shook his head. "Nope," he said decidedly.

Questions I Should Have Asked, #10: Are you *sure* there's nothing you need to tell me? A criminal background or weird proclivities?

We hugged goodbye and I thought, *Well, that wasn't so difficult. He didn't recoil at my admission of bipolar disorder and he didn't have a game-changing revelation.* Relieved and giddy about our upcoming night in the city, I pulled out of the parking lot, my mind already switched to compiling a shopping list for a quick stop at Safeway.

chapter six

ON SATURDAY, we drove across the Bay Bridge and slowly made our way through traffic to the Westin St. Francis on Union Square. I'd never stayed at this hotel. Its name and reputation made it sound so regal. The lobby was beautiful—massive marble columns and detailed ceiling. We found the registration desk and I pulled out my credit card and driver's license, wondering if Larry would suddenly insist on paying for the room or, at least, offer to split the charge. He simply turned around and leaned against the counter to watch the other guests. So much for being a gentleman. I figured it wasn't fair to be annoyed. After all, I'd offered to treat him; I'd proposed the evening in the city.

As we stepped into the elevator, a couple approached, their arms weighed down with two wilting toddlers. Larry held open the door. I smiled sympathetically at the mom who looked like she'd walked the entire forty-seven square, hilly miles of San Francisco. The dad looked less fatigued. I imagined him plotting in his mind: we'll put the kids down for a nap and then have some mom and dad time in the adjacent bed. I remembered those days of traveling with my ex-husband and sons before our divorce. After hours of activity and logistics, hours of catering to others' needs, all I wanted, all I craved was alone-time: an uninterrupted span of quiet, untethered, unmolested time to relax with a book or soak solo in the tub. Sex was never my first choice after one of those long days. That wasn't an indictment on my ex, rather the fact that I, like many women I knew, desperately needed to replenish mentally and physically in my own sacred space. Now, however, I was filled with nervous excitement and an abundance of energy—there was no mantle of fatigue weighing down on me. I couldn't wait to see how Larry and I were together. I kept glancing at him to see if I could detect some nervousness, perhaps some performance anxiety, but his face and body language betrayed nothing.

I waved to one of the little girls as her eyes fluttered in an attempt to stay open. Larry and I followed the signs to our room. After we set our overnight bags on the credenza, I plopped down on the edge of the king-size bed. We had two hours before our dinner reservation. Shopping could wait. My heart was thumping. We were two middle-aged adults whose bodies had undergone decades of wear and tear and were about to be revealed without the benefit of a darkened room or a couple of bottles of champagne. Despite my self-consciousness, I hadn't had sex in years and I was eager to start the christening. It appeared, however, Larry wasn't. He unzipped his backpack and carefully removed the contents, including his tighty-whities. As he opened the top dresser drawer, I thought, *Really? You're doing that now?* I watched in annoyance as he grabbed his toiletries bag and headed to the bathroom. *Maybe he was going to freshen up. Brush away his coffee breath. Should I do the same? I'd just bathed a couple of hours ago.*

"Nice bathroom," he said, reentering the room. He stood at the foot of the bed. "Wanna go do some window shopping before dinner?"

I cocked my head. *Surely, he was joking*, I thought, kicking off my shoes. We were in a hotel room together for the first time and he was thinking about wandering around Union Square and Macy's? I waited for him to laugh off the suggestion. Instead, he reached for his phone and glanced at the display. During the thirteen months Mike and I had dated, we traveled to New York, New Orleans, Santa Barbara, Coronado, Lake Tahoe, Las Vegas, and Whistler. Each time, we'd barely closed the hotel room door and set down the card key before we were tearing at each other's buttons and zippers. Never once had we left a hotel room without some degree of rug burn. But then again, sex had been one of the best and most reliable aspects of our relationship. It was the daily humdrum of the relationship that Mike and I sucked at.

I stared at Larry. He was so fidgety, picking at his nails, checking his cell phone, eyes darting around the room as if looking for a secondary exit. I thought *he's really going to pretend he doesn't know what I was expecting to happen now.*

Determination overrode my feelings of annoyance and hurt. "How about we neck for a bit?" I suggested, figuring that once we started kissing and groping, he'd be overcome with passion. My curiosity was palpable. But more so was my fear. *Maybe he's scared that he'll take one look at my body and can't get an erection? Maybe he's got a tiny dick and thinks I'll swallow him whole? Maybe he's into some kinky shit and he isn't ready to reveal his fetishes? Or maybe he's dealing with intimacy issues because of some childhood abuse?* I'd encountered these issues before. Pretending it didn't matter was often awkward and difficult, and not very genuine.

He set down his cell phone and sat beside me, shoulder to shoulder. Our reflection, two middle-aged adults, stared back at us from the dresser mirror. Awkwardly twisting our necks to face each other, we began kissing. As the kissing became more animated, I suggested we lay down. My body was humming with desire and curiosity as our hands explored each other over our clothes. Laying half on me and half on the mattress, he shifted and accidentally kicked me with his tennis shoe.

"Sorry."

"Why don't you remove your shoes."

"Oh, okay."

As we started kissing again, I felt his crotch, and even through his jeans, I could tell he was becoming aroused. And judging by his bulge, there was sufficient material down there to work with. But minutes later after some enjoyable necking, he pulled away. "Let's head out. I don't want to be late for our dinner reservation."

I knew Larry liked to eat. Most alcoholics I've known, myself included, love sweets, and overindulge in food more than most. It seems that since we'd started dating, his obsession with food had hit overdrive. He had practically orgasmed over my pecan pie, and yet now, he couldn't work up enough desire to lie beside me for ten minutes. It wasn't just that the moment had been ruined, once again, but my doubts about my attractiveness and desirability intensified. I knew, as well, we'd come back to the hotel with our bellies full of Mexican food feeling gassy and less soapy-clean smelling than we were now.

Rather than try to change his mind—there was nothing romantic about begging or pressuring a partner to have sex with you, I adjusted my shirt and said sarcastically, "Let's go do some window shopping. Hate to be late for dinner." If he noticed my disappointment or resentment, it didn't show on his face. We walked to the elevator, nodded hello to a young couple who were emerging from their room with that happy, just-fucked look on their faces, and rode down to the lobby in silence.

A few hours later, with full bellies and tired feet, we rode the elevator up to our room. My mood had improved. The room was darker now that no daylight was peeking through the curtains. I turned on the overhead light in the entry but didn't go around the room flipping on the other switches, as I'm likely to do when traveling with friends. I figured if he was half as uneasy about his body image as I was about mine, it was best to keep the lights low. That way we could ease our way into further revealing ourselves. He set down his phone and peeled off his shoes. Our eyes met and he smiled. I smiled back.

I felt hopeful. It was going to happen. He sat on the edge of the bed and I sat beside him. He said very matter-of-factly, "So . . . should we get to it then?"

Get to it? What the fuck? I've waited all night and months for this? What kind of man says something so crass to a woman? "So . . . should we get to it then," as if he were a bored doctor gloving up to probe one more vagina in a day full of vaginas.

Whatever I'd felt earlier—desire, curiosity, fondness—instantly evaporated. I weighed my options. I could have said, "I'm done. I don't know what your problem is, but I've tried and this isn't working." I could have grabbed my purse and suitcase and left him to entertain himself. I could have kicked him out of the room, letting him ride BART home, and then ordered a pot of tea, dessert, and a pay-per-view movie. We could have both left, although it was too late to get a refund on the room and endure the uneasy silence on the drive home.

I straightened my back, took a deep breath. The idea of going home to an empty house seemed more depressing than sleeping next to Mr. Get To It, Larry. Even if that was all it turned out to be—sleeping. He placed a hand on my knee. I looked at him and asked myself: *What do you see in this guy? Sure, he's nice, but do you* really *want someone who seems so indifferent toward getting to know you better? Or are you that lonely?*

"Want to watch a movie?" I asked.

He smiled and removed his hand from my knee. "Yeah. Sure."

From the relief on his face, one might have thought a surgeon had just removed a cantaloupe-size tumor from his balls and determined the mass benign. I wanted to smack him. I went into the bathroom to slip on my nightgown, grabbed a bottled water from the minibar, and tossed another to Larry. We flipped through the movie selections until we agreed on "Juno." I'd seen it several times; I loved the witty dialog. As we sat in bed—Larry in his sweatpants and me in my nightgown, we held hands and laughed at gems like the scene where Juno tells her dad and stepmom that she's pregnant, dashing their hopes that the news was simply a drug habit or expulsion from school. I loved watching the unexpected friendship develop between Juno and the adoptive-father-to-be. It never failed to disgust me when they're slow dancing in his living room and he announces he's leaving his wife for Juno—a girl barely half his age. How could the character delude himself into thinking this young girl would have any interest in a middle-aged man-child? Ironically, Larry could have offered his perspective on the situation had I known then his predilection for young girls.

As the credits rolled, Larry leaned in for a kiss, and finally, his hand slipped beneath my nightgown. His fumbling became more urgent and we had sex. He didn't come. He blamed it on being out of practice and nervous.

Questions I Should Have Asked, #11: Are you sure that's the real reason? Is this something that works itself out over time?

I knew there was a lot of pressure on guys to perform, especially the first time with someone new, so I wasn't alarmed. Next time, I figured. So what if the sex was a bit bland? I was happy that he could sustain an impressive erection and was happy to let me get on top so I could climax. In the morning, we had sex again. It was similarly bland as the evening before, and again, he wasn't able to reach orgasm. To his credit, he was tender and pleasing and amply endowed.

chapter seven

IT HAD BEEN A few weeks since Larry and I had gone for our over-night in San Francisco. My friend Lynne and I were walking around the lower trail of the Lafayette Reservoir, as we had been doing for years. As we passed moms herding their young kids and older couples holding hands or moved aside to let packs of joggers run past, we took turns updating each other on our art and writing. Difficulties with our children or exes. Financial worries. Book and movie recommendations. The most interesting, graphic, and lively topic was always our boyfriends—current and former.

Lynne agreed with most of my friends that Larry was really nice, but egregiously boring and unimaginative. The only ambition he'd shown was signing on with Jane to flip houses. "But," I argued. "He's like a worn but comfortable pair of slippers that you just can't toss out. And, he doesn't drink or have any STDs."

Lynne shook her head and asked, "Is that how low you've set the bar?"

I laughed. She was right. "Guess if it were any lower, I'd be tripping over it."

"You know, that's a pathetic reason for continuing to see him. Don't you want to have amazing sex? Be in a relationship with some-one who stimulates you intellectually?"

"Well, Mike and I had amazing sex. Look at where that got me. But you're right," I admitted. "I never imagined as a young girl that finding my prince charming would come down whether or not he had STDs."

What I enjoyed and appreciated most about Lynne was that we could say anything to each other. We could always find the humor in even the most difficult situations or our worst behavior. We cared enough about each other to give honest feedback and advice.

"He finally had an orgasm." I stepped off the path to let a pair of joggers pass.

"Really? Wow!"

"Yeah. We'd slept in and I was expecting Jane to ring the doorbell at any minute to go to lunch. We'd started having sex and I told him that if he planned to finish, he had five minutes before Jane arrived. Somehow, it seemed the idea of getting caught or running out of time helped push him over the edge."

"So, he can do it now?"

"I'm not sure. It may have just been a one-off. There's been no repeat performance." I laughed and rolled my eyes.

After a few months of dating, I asked my sons if they were okay with Larry sleeping over. The first night, before bedtime, Zack laid at the foot of my bed reading one of his books while Larry and I lounged in our pajamas. I read the newspaper and Larry read a paperback novel. It felt like a family again. Since Mike, I had missed having a man in the house. Someone lying next to me at night to chat with and share the newspaper.

Reading the newspaper and working the daily Sudoku puzzle was the best conclusion to my hectic days. When my sons were younger, they'd be fully engrossed in Legos or a game, and the moment I climbed in bed to read the newspaper, they'd hear that familiar pop of the rubber band, run over, and start nudging me to entertain them. They were like our cats, Toby and Shelby, in that way. The sounds of me unfolding the newspaper was an invitation to jump on my bed and nuzzle their wet noses between me and the paper. For years, between the boys and the cats, reading the newspaper quietly, undisturbed, was a futile, frustrating undertaking. But now, the boys had accepted that bedtime was my reading time. No longer did they constantly pull me out of a story with questions like, "Why does that lady look so weird?" or "Look at all those guns! Are they bad guys?" I got to enjoy my favorite columnists, like Amy Alkon and Tony Hicks, in peace.

Larry, I found, was a very compatible reading partner. We'd slide under my double layer of goose down comforters in our pajamas, and he'd read a crime novel while I made my way through the newspaper, starting with the above-the-fold headlines and then peeling back the pages, one by one. Larry liked to read the sales inserts and cartoons, neither of which interested me, so I was happy to set those aside in case he lost interest in his novel. Sometimes he'd surprise me and pick up a section once I'd finished, but only after I'd finished. He wasn't one of those people who'd grab someone else's paper, start pulling apart the sections until the order was so fucked up that it became a scavenger hunt to find the second half of a story. Sometimes I'd share a headline or an article I thought might amuse or shock him, especially if I had some personal connection to the person quoted or featured in an article. He'd dog-ear the page of his novel and listen patiently.

The Advice Goddess, Amy Alkon, had been one of Mike and my favorite columnists. Her philosophy was Take No Prisoners. She held nothing back in her responses and spared no feelings. Her column was like a salty-sweet dessert after the main course. If it was an especially good column, I'd say to Larry, "Listen to this one . . ." He never complained, never hurried me to finish the paper saying he had to wake up early the next day or wanted to make love before he fell asleep. In fact, he always left the decision of whether to make love or not to me.

He seemed happy enough to oblige or forgo. There was never any pressure. It was so easy.

Questions I Should Have Asked, #12: Are you fine with always letting me decide whether we have sex or go to sleep?

A month or so later, we were sitting in bed and he'd dozed off while I read the paper. I flipped the page to Amy Alkon's column. I read the first line. It sounded familiar. I read the line again and then the second. *Holy shit. It couldn't be.* I folded the paper and glanced at Larry to see if he'd detected a change in the air. His eyes were closed. He was making his gurgling, snoring sound. I angled away so that if he woke up and glanced over, he wouldn't see which section I was on and ask, "What's Amy got to say tonight?"

I'd written to Amy for advice after Larry and my night away in San Francisco. I figured it was a longshot that she'd actually respond and publish my letter. I wanted an unbiased perspective since Jane's loyalty seemed too flexible and Lynne, of course, sided with me. I read her response and suppressed my giggles. What I loved about Amy was that she was smart, brutally honest, and had apparently read every psychology book ever published.

Dear Amy,

I'm a 46-year-old woman who just started seeing a 55-year-old man. He's always telling me how excited I get him, how he's your typical horny male, and how I'm asking for trouble if we make out at the door after lunch. Frankly, he seems all talk. For example, on our much-anticipated weekend away in San Francisco, we had two hours to kill at the hotel before dinner. He suggested window shopping. I suggested we "make out on the bed." (I wanted to say "have wild sex.") We kissed, and when things started heating up, he said we should head out. When we returned, he said, "So, should we get to it then?" It was so crass I suggested a movie. He seemed relieved, and we watched "Juno." Afterward, we started fooling around, but it was bland — as was sex the next morning. I'm frustrated but hoping things will improve over time. Am I too focused on sex? I should say something, but it's so awkward, and I don't want to hurt his feelings.

— Lustbucket

I cringed. *Where in the hell did she come up with the name Lustbucket?*

Dear Lustbucket,

Here you are on a weekend getaway with a guy you just started seeing, and all he can think to do is get away from the bed: "Shall we totter down to Neiman Marcus and stare at the displays?" Now, there is that chance he's freezing up out of performance anxiety or because he sees sleeping together as an I.O.U. for commitment. But more than likely, his favorite sex positions are spooning, snoring, and doggie-style—as in rolling over and playing dead.

This sort of bedroom bait-and-switch – the dud billing himself as a dynamo – is pretty common with older guys who are embarrassed that they don't want sex like they used to. Perhaps this guy's had a drop in his testosterone level (as men do, usually after 40), or perhaps there never was much "T" to go around. What's especially worrisome is that this brand-new relationship—the time when you should be having trouble making it out of the elevator with clothes on. In "The Truth About Love," Dr. Patricia Love explains, "During infatuation, with the help of PEA (phenethylamine), dopamine, and norepinephrine, the person with the low sex drive (the low-T person) experiences a surge in sexual desire." Uh-oh. What's he experiencing, a surge in window shopping?

As for whether you're "too focused on sex," you are what you are—*probably too focused on it to be satisfied with a guy who'd rather watch "Juno" than ... you know ... but who finally blurts out, "So, should we get to it then?" What, clean the hog pen? Yeah, let's get this chore over with. You can hint a guy into expressing himself more appealingly, but what matters is whether that's how he really feels: if he'd really rather be napping.*

You hear people say stuff like, "Sex is best in the context of a loving relationship." No, sex is best when the two people having it are sexually compatible. You can ask a guy to do more of what you like, but you can't get him to be more of what you like. Go ahead, hang around a little longer, maybe try initiating, and see whether he's just a bit slow to come out of hibernation. Ultimately, the person in need of your honesty is you: whether the man for you is one who's always got Mr. Happy at the ready, or whether you can make do with a guy who should probably pet-name his entire sex drive Nuclear Winter.

Amy Alkon, 2008

I slid the page into my nightstand drawer to read again the next day. Larry laid next to me as still as a hibernating bear. Perhaps he felt my eyes on him, because suddenly he opened his and my head nearly hit the ceiling. He sleepily asked if I was finished with the paper. I could smell his breath and leaned away. I felt guilty that I'd betrayed him. I was certain, as I took a sip of my water, if he looked hard enough, he'd see the shame on my face, and maybe a bit of giddiness—my letter had made the cut and was published in a nationally syndicated advice column! I knew it was a million to one chance he'd ever read or hear about the column. I wondered if Mike would read it and recognize my writing. If so, would he think fondly of me and our many hotel stays?

If Larry happened to read the article, would he recognize us? I wondered. Amy had attributed the letter to Lustbucket. I'd never refer to myself in such unflattering terms. Juno was, unfortunately, a pretty unique detail. Each detail by themselves might be easy to overlook, but put together the location, our ages, and his "So, should we get to it then," it was specifically familiar.

Later, out of courtesy, I emailed an early draft of this memoir to Larry in prison while he was serving his fifteen-year sentence. I figured I'd give him an opportunity to challenge or correct anything I had written. This would be, presumably, the first he'd learn of my letter to Amy. I had not set out to publicly humiliate or hurt him, but my published letter would certainly do so.

chapter eight

I HAD A SOFTBALL FRIEND, April, who struggled with depression. Another friend and I had visited her in a psychiatric hospital after one of her suicide attempts. Over the years I'd known her and played ball together, I'd spent hours, as had other close friends, on the phone listening to her tales of hopelessness. I'd given her one pep talk after another. But her struggles were getting more severe. Her therapist kept threatening to have her placed on seventy-two-hour hold. She wanted April to consider shock treatments. She increased her number of group therapy sessions and switched her meds.

When April was in a stable place, she was a really funny, sweet woman. She could laugh at herself and her situation. At a group camping, she told me about one of her suicide attempts where she'd swallowed a bottle of Lamictal (the same medicine I took for my bipolar). Rather than kill herself, she'd gotten extremely sick—barfing and crawling her way across the carpet to call for an ambulance. Even though it was a serious subject, the way she described crawling across the floor left us both holding our sides, laughing. (I made a mental note: Never attempt an overdose with Lamictal. Barfing is the absolute worst. It always felt like someone was ripping out your insides with plyers.)

Unfortunately, for April, stability was a fickle, unreliable guest. On a Tuesday night, our softball team went to Mountain Mike's after our game for pizza and beer. Nothing about her behavior that evening stuck out. Larry and I had driven her home. She seemed upbeat. Not great, never great, but okay for April. We had laughed about running into each other at Safeway the past Sunday after a pickup softball game and flirting with some firefighters who were doing their grocery shopping. I had hoped one of the guys would take an interest in April and ask her out. Four days later, on Saturday, Larry was working on a handyman project at my house. Austin and Zack were in the living room playing video games. I was writing in my office when my cell phone rang. It was Brian, one of our teammates.

"I have some awful news. I think April committed suicide."

"What do you mean, you *think*?"

"We got a call from the apartment manager. We were listed as emergency contacts. The guy said that he let the police into her apartment. They've taken her away."

"Where'd they take her? To the morgue or a hospital? Was she alive?"

"I don't know. The man was kind of vague. I tried calling the morgue, but they wouldn't give me any information."

"I could try calling. Do you have the number?"

I went to my bedroom to make the call. My mind couldn't settle on an image. April may or may not have killed herself. Either she was in a hospital, possibly hooked up to tubes and machines, or she was on a cold table in a morgue. It didn't seem real. We'd just played softball. Maybe this was just another failed attempt. Hopefully, she wasn't dead, but merely recovering in the hospital, waiting to be stabilized and returned to the psych ward. When I got through to the morgue, I asked if they had a person by the name of April Jones there. "I'm a close friend."

"Yes, we have her body."

"So, you're saying she's dead."

"That is correct."

"And just to make sure we're talking about the same person, I'm calling about April Jones."

"Yes, that is correct. Who did you say is calling?"

"A friend. So, she's dead?"

"Yes."

I hung up the phone and sat on my bed, stunned, before succumbing to tears. I found Larry in the kitchen. He set down his measuring tape when he saw my face. The boys were playing video games, so until they heard me crying and saw Larry hugging me, they didn't know that something bad had happened. Larry held me tight, kept me upright, as I said, "April's dead. She killed herself." He was so compassionate. It couldn't have been faked.

When I dated Mike, it had always surprised me that for such an unabashed romantic man, he could be so emotionless, so detached when faced with another's suffering. He loved the chase, apparently more than the prize. He was constantly buying me flowers. He wrote mushy cards and poems. I'd find notes on my pillow and in my car. Everything signed, "I love you, all ways and always." We were high on our love for each other. Kissing and constantly touching like sixteen-year-olds. Yet toward the end of our relationship, when I could feel him pulling away despite his increasingly defensive and angry assurances that he wasn't, I nosedived into a heavy depression.

One day we sat at the top of his driveway under the eve of the carport. I was trying to explain, through my sobs, how sad I felt. We were knee lengths apart. Mike sat with his hands folded in his lap, not saying anything, not making an overture to comfort me. He looked worried that the neighbors could see him and his hysterical girlfriend from their kitchen window. Imagining this, his utmost worry, I cried even harder as he remained as rigid and cold as the cement under us. I told him I felt so lonely. The fun in our relationship had morphed into drama—and he hadn't signed on for drama.

Larry was a different sort of boyfriend. Flowers and cards weren't his thing. Poetry? Had he even written a poem since assigned by some middle or high school teacher? Probably not. Unlike Mike, he didn't make far off plans and promises: romantic notions that sounded great in theory and sparkled under the warm, glowing light of new love, but soon dimmed to a cold, impenetrable nothingness. The passion that Mike and I had felt was probably a once in a lifetime event. Larry was simply steady. Boring but steady. And being with him was better, most days, than being alone.

April's father contacted me about helping him clean out her apartment. Larry drove me to the airport to pick him up. He played chauffeur as we helped the man make arrangements and sort out the car rental. He listened to me when I described the surreal, sad experience of helping a father clean out his daughter's apartment. He listened as I recounted all the details of the day—seeing that one of the curtain rods had been eerily yanked from the wall; learning from her father she'd hung herself by tying a rope to the front doorknob (I didn't even know that such a thing was possible.). I described how I'd tossed out the wilted green and red caps of the strawberries left in her sink, washed the single wine glass she'd last drank from and offered to mail the Netflix movie envelop for her father—and later peeked inside to see that April had rented, but not watched, "The Bucket List."

There was so much good in Larry that later it would be difficult to reconcile *this* Larry with the *other* Larry.

chapter nine

IN MY HEART, I've tried to believe that people strive to be good. Good to others. Good to themselves (but not at the expense of others). And good to me. That people are decent and caring. I'm not some Pollyanna. There are those who prove, again and again, to be the antithesis of caring, loving, and trusting. However, my ability to judge accurately a person's trustworthiness has been on the fritz my entire life. Repeatedly, people who were supposed to care for me, protect me, love me proved untrustworthy, even heartless. Despite the accumulation of evidence, I still often convinced myself that *this time* would be different. If I tried harder at being good, clever, smart, pretty, perhaps I could trust that someone would eventually think I was worthy of doing right by. So often, my assessment of a situation, when shared with others, was disputed, refuted, or rewarded with punishment or scorn or bemusement that I was left questioning my perceptions.

I had dated a man in San Francisco during graduate school. One night after many drinks with friends, he invited me back to his house. While we lay in bed after having sex, I could see inside his open closet. His bedroom was tiny—I could easily reach the closet door if I stretched my arm. In the closet, hanging among a few suits and dress shirts, was a pink nightgown. *That's odd*, I thought. Surely there was a reason that a pink nightgown was hanging in his closet. If he had had something to hide, he'd actually try hiding it. He wouldn't have left his closet door ajar. As he dozed off, I remembered he'd mentioned his sister had visited the previous weekend. *That's it*, I told myself. *The nightgown belonged to his sister. She had simply forgotten it.*

A few weeks later, over dinner, he said that we needed to talk. It turned out he had a fiancé in Sacramento. Because of an ugly argument between him and her father months earlier, his fiancé was waiting for tensions to relax before they proceeded with the wedding plans. I was completely shocked.

"Then why did you invite me out if you were engaged?"

He shrugged. "I thought, what's the harm? One dinner out? But then you had plans for the next two weekends—traveling here and then there. It became a challenge to see if I could get a date with you. Then, it turned out I liked you."

I was a challenge to conquer? What a dick! The pink nightgown popped into my head.

"Was that her nightgown hanging in your closet?"

"I wondered why you didn't say anything. I knew there was no way you hadn't noticed it." He laughed when I told him I had assumed it was his sister's. "And the tampons under the sink, my aunt's?"

I smiled and thought, okay, let's not get carried away. But, had I rooted around under his sink and discovered a box of tampons, I'm may or may not have assured myself there was a plausible explanation like they'd been left behind by his roommate's former girlfriend.

After my sons finished their school year, Larry invited us to join him on a camping trip with Jane and his volleyball friends—some, like Jane, he'd had considered close friends and hung out with for twenty-plus years. I was excited. I'd finally meet these people whom I'd known only by name until this point. Larry drove up first to set up our two tents and inflate our air mattresses so that when we arrived, our accommodations would be perfect. We spent the next five days on the Eel River in Northern California barbecuing, chatting around the fire, making s'mores, and playing volleyball while the next generation of toddlers ran around half-naked. One night the grownups were talking about how scary it was to drive late at night when you're exhausted and sleepy. How sometimes you tell yourself, I'll just close my eyes for one second and the next thing you knew, you'd drifted off the road and were awakened by the clunk, clunk, clunk sound of your tires hitting the rumble strips. My remedy, I told them, was to blast the music or open the window so that the entire car vibrated with either bass or wind, and in dire situations, both. One of Larry's friends shared his proven method for staying awake and avoiding a collision: masturbation. Whenever he was sleepy and driving alone at night, he'd reach into his pants and have a go. I couldn't believe he was sharing this information with his friends and one of his friend's new girlfriend—me and my sons. I kept picturing the man's messy hands and wondered where he had wiped them afterward and what his steering wheel would look like under one of those infrared crime-scene lights. If it weren't for my sons sitting next to me looking shocked by the man's admission, I might have encouraged him to reveal more crazy facts about himself. The conversation, luckily, steered down a different road.

Shortly after the camping trip, I saw an ad for a Cher concert. She was performing in Las Vegas, and even though I hated Las Vegas, I knew that Cher was getting up in age and I might not have many more opportunities to watch her perform live and see her crazy costumes.

"Do you want to go to Las Vegas?" I asked Larry one day when he stopped by for lunch. "I know you were just there for your birthday, but I really want to see Cher." He hesitated. I figured he might be too embarrassed to admit another trip wasn't in his budget. "My treat," I whispered. My housekeeper, who was cleaning in the living room, didn't like Larry, so I didn't want her to overhear me. She complained that he was a mooch—always eating at my house and never bringing groceries. It also pissed her off that he didn't buy me flowers like Mike had done each month on our anniversaries. I tried to convince her I didn't mind about the flowers, and argued that for my birthday, he'd gotten me a nice softball glove and bat bag.

I made the arrangements, and at dinner that evening, I told my sons about the upcoming trip. I didn't mention that I was paying for the entire weekend (airfare, hotel, food, taxies), because they'd heard me regularly complain about money. Given the stock market and housing implosion, I was constantly cautioning the boys that we needed to watch our spending. At dinner, after assuring the boys that Las Vegas wasn't really a city for kids and that we'd do something else later in the summer, I asked Larry which of his volleyball friends was it that he went to Las Vegas with for his birthday. Now that I'd met most of them, I had faces to go with the names and stories.

Larry stopped mid-bite and looked at me. His green eyes were perfectly still. "Let's talk about this later," he mumbled.

"What's wrong?"

He shook his head. "We'll talk after dinner."

I was determined to find out what he was not telling me. "I just want to know who was on the trip since I've met your buddies."

"Not now. Please." He looked terrified. Whatever it was, I realized I didn't want to discover in front of my sons.

"Okay." I smiled. Curiosity and confusion whirled around my head. Something was up. I was going to find out as soon as I could scarf down dinner and drag Larry to my bedroom for a private conversation.

We sat on the edge of my bed with the door closed. His quiet, nervous demeanor was starting to concern me. "So, who did you go on the trip with? Was it Don and Rodney?" They were the most likely candidates.

"Remember that woman I was dating right before you?"

"Yeah, the one you broke up with before you called me for a walk."

"Technically, yes."

"*Technically, yes?* What does that mean?"

"See, we'd bought the tickets and booked the hotel months earlier before you and I had become intimate. I didn't want to just cancel on her."

"Instead, you lied to me."

"We didn't have sex." His Adam's apple rose and fell. "I promise."

"Right. Then you had separate rooms?"

"No, but—"

"Did you share a bed?

"Well, yes."

"You shared a bed but somehow managed not to have sex the entire weekend while sleeping side by side?"

He traced a seam in the comforter, up a few inches and then back to its starting place. Up and then back. "She's not interested in having sex with me."

Okay. That was semi-plausible. He probably hadn't had much luck in climaxing with her either.

"Besides, she was drunk half the time."

"Why wouldn't you tell me instead of lying?" I asked. "Didn't you think I'd eventually meet your friends and ask?"

"I hoped you'd forget and it wouldn't come up. I just didn't want it to become a big deal between us because I was really starting to like you."

"You have a funny way of showing it." I thought about who I could invite to Las Vegas in his place. Lynne didn't travel much for pleasure since she often traveled for craft shows. A weekend with Jane would be a weekend all about Jane, and sometimes that was too much to endure. My softball friends and I had started pulling away; I didn't feel especially close to my teammates anymore. Larry's airplane ticket was nonrefundable and non-exchangeable, so even if I uninvited him, the ticket couldn't be transferred to another friend. Scrapping the entire trip meant throwing away money, especially money I'd spent on the Cher concert tickets.

"No more lying," I said. "Got it?"

He picked at his thumbnail and said, "I promise."

Questions I Should Have Asked, #13: What else has he lied about or hidden from me?

Was he shocked that I forgave him so easily? I hadn't really. I didn't tell him then, but after catching him in this needless lie, I knew without a doubt that there was little chance of me falling madly in love with him as I had with Mike. He was a liar and a coward. But I wanted to see Cher, and he was, mostly, a comfortable companion. Sometimes he was crass. Listening to his handyman stories was still as boring as listening to a dishwasher run through its cycles. He watched a lot of television. But on the plus side, my sons didn't hate him. I never worried that I wasn't smart enough for him, or pretty enough, or sophisticated enough. I supposed I always felt superior to him and this must have provided me some level of satisfaction. I didn't have to put on airs or worry about my grammar or try to impress him with the books I'd read, countries I'd visited, because who was Larry to judge me? And even though he still only once reached a climax with me, and he was more talk than action in the bedroom, he never left me unfulfilled.

So, I'd caught him in a lie. I rationalized that as long as I didn't catch a disease from him or this ex-girlfriend, I was willing to overlook one lie and another character flaw. I did, however, call Jane the next day to ask if she had known about Larry and the ex-girlfriend going to Las Vegas for his birthday.

"Yes," she'd said. "But I made him swear to tell you about his plans."

"He didn't."

"Well, he claimed he did. And I believed him."

"Why didn't you ever mention it to me? Ask if I was really okay with Larry and his ex-girlfriend sharing a hotel room?"

"I wanted to respect your privacy. I figured if you wanted to talk about it, you'd bring it up." *When had privacy ever been an issue between us?* I wanted to ask. She'd shared the most intimate details of her sex life with both Larry and me. She'd recently come over for a surprise visit, and in front of Larry, unzipped my hoodie to see if I was wearing a t-shirt or bra, and then laughed at my shock when she realized I wasn't wearing anything underneath and my boobs were now on full display. I'd say we were on pretty intimate terms.

"You know that if the situation had been reversed and I'd known and not told you that your new boyfriend was going on a weekend rendezvous to Las Vegas with his ex, you'd be pissed. Am I right?"

Questions I Should Have Asked, #14: What else are you not telling me about Larry's past?

The thing with Jane was that I could never get her to admit she was wrong. I'd never hear her say, "I'm sorry. You're right. I should have looked out for my friend." As furious as I was at that moment, I chalked it up to her narcissistic tendencies. If she needed something from me, she'd be at my doorstep or on the phone immediately. Jane did as Jane wanted; Jane followed her moral compass wherever it led her. If there was something I needed, I'd usually have to wait until it was convenient for her. Not always. Sometimes, she surprised me, and I think that was what kept me from abandoning our friendship.

Larry and I arrived in Las Vegas on Friday. Midday Saturday, we were resting by the pool, reading and enjoying the warm weather despite the overhead clouds of cigarette smoke. I received a text saying that Cher's concert had been canceled due to illness.

"What the fuck!"

I showed Larry the message which he shrugged off saying, "Oh, well." I rolled my eyes, and thought about all the money I'd spend on airfare, hotel, meals, taxies, etc., just to see her perform and she'd canceled.

In the cab that evening after dinner, I told the driver about the canceled concert and asked if he had any suggestions for alternate entertainment, something we wouldn't find at home in Walnut Creek. He listed a few shows that were playing around town. A couple I'd seen, the others I wasn't willing to pay last-minute prices to see. After a few moments of silence, the driver looked at us in the rearview mirror.

"There are sex clubs you could check out."

"Really," I asked, immediately thinking of Tom Cruise in *Eyes Wide Shut* when he sneaks into a secret society's masked orgy. Despite the creepiness of the film, it provided a shocking yet intriguing peek inside a warped, surreal world. "Do you have to participate, or can you just watch?"

"I think you can do whatever you want," he said.

"Watching might be entertaining," I said. "Or at least interesting." Larry was quiet. He looked at the window as we drove down the strip. "Are those places clean? I wouldn't want to catch a disease or crabs by accidentally brushing up against someone or something."

"They are probably regulated. They must be required to meet some sort of health code standards," the driver said.

"No way." Larry let go of my hand and folded his arms like a belligerent child. "I don't want to watch a bunch of strangers have sex. That's disgusting."

Questions I Should Have Asked, #15: Are you telling me you've never watched porn?

"Oh, come on. You're such a prude."

"Go without me if you want," he said, refusing to look at me.

"I'm not going to a sex club by myself," I said. "Let's just go for five minutes and then we'll leave."

"Nope."

"It would be funny. Just five minutes. And don't worry, I'll pay the admission."

"I'd rather go back to the hotel and watch a movie."

Of course, you would, I thought, resenting him for not being any fun. He refused to make even the tiniest attempt at being something more than the most boring man in the universe. Sitting in the cab, silently fuming, I couldn't understand his reluctance, his lack of curiosity. Even boring assholes must have some curiosity. *Why couldn't he just humor me for a few minutes? After all, I'd paid for this whole fucking trip. Couldn't we have one amusing memory from an otherwise disappointing trip?*

"Have you ever seen ordinary people have sex before?" I asked. He ignored my question. "It's really kind of funny. I once saw a drunk British couple in Greece having the worst sex on a pier. The girl kept nudging the guy to wake up, and his knees kept buckling under her weight. Aren't you curious to see what kind of people actually frequent these places?"

"Not at all."

"It's not as if we'd be the ones doing something immoral," I whispered. "We'd only be spectators."

"So, what will it be?" the driver asked.

"The hotel," Larry said.

I sat there thinking *what a boring prude.* And yet, I was dating him.

chapter ten

AS A RESULT OF the bipolar meds and the antidepressants I had been taking for the five years since Mike and I broke up, I'd steadily gained weight. I had worked so hard to lose the weight after my divorce, and now I was stacking up pound after pound. My psychiatrist had prescribed a different antidepressant that claimed not to cause weight gain as a side effect. A couple of weeks after starting these new meds, I could feel the depression storming back into my body. With Austin and Zack to look after, my worry about finances, and everything else I had going on, I didn't have time to see if the new antidepressant would eventually start working. I'd have to switch back to Prozac, thus leading, most likely, to more weight gain.

Larry was in my backyard with his helper Jose installing a massive twelve thousand dollar above-ground pool that I'd bought on a whim during a heatwave. So much for living within our means. Larry's one-week, "It'll be fun and easy!" project had turned into weeks of frustration, and thousands of dollars more than he'd estimated for his and Jose's time. Plus, free home-cooked lunches that I explained to my housekeeper were my way of keeping him on my property and focused on finishing a pool—a pool that looked as if it belonged in a trailer park.

There were days I'd come home after grocery shopping or running errands and find him on my computer. He'd startle and say that he was looking something up on YouTube—some video on wiring or plumbing. I'd cringe. I knew the internet had become a great resource for do-it-yourselfers, but Larry had been in construction for decades. Shouldn't he already know how to wire and plumb shit? Twice, I overheard him calling his electrician friend for advice. I listened to him explain a problem he had encountered, and I nearly had heart tremors. Sure, accountants ask other accountants for help and second opinions, but we all know the basics—our debits from credits, what entries hit the Balance Sheet versus the Income Statement. Every day, I kept asking myself, what in the hell had I signed up for?

When the pool was nearing completion, Larry tapped into the wiring outside my office to run the equipment and new outdoor lights. I checked to see how things were coming along with the trenches he and Jose were digging.

"Is that deep enough," I asked, looking at the shallow open trenches. "Seems like they should be lower than an inch down."

"It should be fine." He wiped the sweat from his face. He'd grown a goatee at my suggestion and it improved his looks tenfold. He looked more rugged in a Harrison Ford kind of way. The next time I went outside to check on his progress, I saw that he'd laid the electrical wires in the trenches. At the intersections, where the wires would fan out in different directions—from the new light posts to the pool equipment to the circuit box, he'd begun splicing the wires together. I kneeled down and inspected his work. The PVC pipes were cut inches from each intersection and the naked wires were sticking out. They had been spliced and joined and capped in little red plastic hats and lay in the shallow dirt trench.

"I'm not an electrician," I said, "but burying unprotected wire without some sort of watertight box doesn't seem safe." He looked at Jose. Jose looked at his dirty work boots. I raised my eyebrows. "You're not going to electrocute the boys and me?" I laughed half-heartedly.

"Seriously, it seems as if the wires should have some sort of little box to protect them from water."

"This is standard. I looked it up online and checked with a couple of friends."

How reassuring, I thought. *I've met your friends. Was one of these friends the masturbator?* The next morning before Larry and Jose arrived, I checked on the wiring. The sprinklers had run a couple of hours earlier. And now, the wires were laying in puddles of water. The little red hat looks like they were swimming in muddy pools.

What the fuck? I thought, my heart beating with disbelief and anger. *He's got to be kidding? He's going to electrocute my sons and their friends who were always playing in the backyard and digging holes for their BMX ramps. Their parents would surely sue me to high heaven!*

I called Mark, my regular handyman and long-time friend, to come over and give me his expert opinion. Larry arrived midmorning and found Mark and me standing over one of the trenches, huddled in disbelief. I introduced Larry to Mark and explained that I wasn't trying to hurt his feelings or undermine him, but I needed some reassurance about the wiring. He wouldn't even make eye contact with me. I'm sure he was humiliated. How could he not be? He had failed at something he claimed would be so easy, and now I had to pay someone more expensive to correct his work. While Mark corrected the wiring, Larry and Jose laid the cement pad for the pool equipment. I was so tempted to offer to pay Mark and his guys whatever it took to finish the job correctly. Just to be done with it. Lesson learned. Never trust Larry to build anything again. But I couldn't afford Mark's rates. Yet even at Larry's rates, I was still facing an additional two thousand dollars to see the job completed, if not more.

After writing Mark a check for his work, I walked him to his truck. "I've lost all confidence in Larry. This might sound harsh, but he's a fucking idiot."

Mark laughed. "Well, he's your boyfriend." He smiled and I sighed. "It'll be fine. Call me once he's got the electrical panel in. I'll swing by to look it over."

I walked back to where Larry was working, replaying Mark's barb, "Well, he's your boyfriend," and decided that I'd had enough of Larry's incompetence. "I need to know when you're going to be done," I said. "I'm really, really panicking. I know you don't mean to, but it feels like you're taking advantage of me. If I see you check the internet one more time to get electrical or plumbing advice, I'm going to lose it. It looks like a trailer-park back here. I can't afford to bring down my home value."

He admitted that the project had become more involved and complicated than he'd estimated. It wouldn't have surprised me if he'd added, "Well, fuck it. If Mark's so great, let him finish the pool and lights." But he simply said, "For the sake of our relationship, maybe it's best you don't hire me to do any more projects around your house."

Geez. That's all you have for me? For the sake of our relationship. This was not the assurance I was hoping for.

"You are going to finish, right?"

He nodded. The look on his face betrayed him. I started crying. Jose pretended not to eavesdrop or watch as I stood in my backyard a few yards away sobbing. Perhaps he'd seen this before with Larry and his frustrated clients. Jane had recently complained that Larry wasn't quite the skilled handyman she'd once believed. Once again, this information was only relayed after I'd hired him.

Larry held me tightly as I cried. Through tears, I admitted that I needed to go back to Prozac but was worried about how much more weight and stress my body could handle before the needle moved from pre-diabetic to diabetic. And managing diabetes would mean expensive testing strips and insulin. I was already spending two hundred dollars a month on antidepressants and my bipolar prescription and another four hundred on therapy—none of which I paid through my insurance for fear they'd cancel me as a high risk.

Standing in my backyard, crying in Larry's arms, everything suddenly felt like too much—the pool fiasco, increasing financial worries, switching meds, the weight gain. Larry held and soothed me. Unlike Mike, he didn't tell me I had more than enough money and I was worrying about nothing. He didn't get defensive and claim that I was blaming him when I was the one who hired him to build a pool, even though he'd never built one before. He didn't seize the opportunity to lecture me on my weight or speculate that surely not everyone on Prozac finds it impossible to maintain or lose weight.

In fact, not once during our thirteen months of dating had Larry put pressure on me to look a certain way, to fit a particular mold, to trade my granny panties for thongs. He never asked me to wear contacts rather than glasses or to wear my hair, imbued with a greenish tint from diving, one way versus another. Sure, he liked Jane's floral sundresses, especially the low necklines. She always attempted to look nice, wearing mascara and styling her hair. It was obvious to anyone standing next to Larry and Jane that he had a school-boy crush on her. I wasn't jealous or threatened. I never felt the need to compete with her for his affection. I never feared losing Larry to her or someone like her. She'd made it clear when I teased her, in his absence, about his obvious crush that she was way out of his league. She had no interest in Larry in *that* way. I think she enjoyed having her Loyal Larry Fan Club. It fed her ego, especially between boyfriends.

Even though he understood that for health reasons, it was important I try to keep my weight down. I don't think that an increase or decrease of twenty pounds swayed his affection toward me. Jane had shared that a major issue in Larry's marriage had been his lack of attention to his wife—and from all reports, she was an attractive woman. It wasn't particularly flattering to know, or strongly suspect, that he looked upon my outward beauty, or lack thereof, with similar indifference. To his credit, he never made me feel self-conscious about how I dressed for comfort over fashion. He never remarked on the portions of food I served myself or ate in restaurants. He never lectured me when I ate pralines; we both knew brown sugar and butter weren't on a pre-diabetic diet.

He never overwhelmed me with flattery: "Oh, you're so beautiful. You look gorgeous. You're so hot!"

Questions I Should Have Asked, #16: What exactly is *your* type? Do you even find me attractive?

He wasn't like Mike and others—he didn't feed me constant adorations and compliments, encourage me to dine greedily on this buffet of affection, and then, without warning, slammed the lid shut. He'd never made false promises, especially not, "I love you for all ways and always." He never burrowed his way into my heart, made his presence feel so vital to my wellbeing that once he was gone, I'd feel his absence so acutely. He never looked so deeply I'd needed to worry that under close examination he could detect the unforgivable flaws that were mine, and mine alone. He was a less than desirable boyfriend in many ways, but I knew that there were some redeeming or at least benign aspects of him. And in truth, I never looked that closely. I didn't probe too deeply into his childhood, his being orphaned as a teenager, his divorce, his past cancer, his coaching days, his past relationship, his apparent secrets, his fetishes, his morals, his bucket list. I never asked, "What's the most embarrassing thing hanging in your closet?" I just wasn't that curious. He seemed an open and shut case—a man who, between the covers of Larry Pallen's file, nothing of interest ever did or would happen.

chapter eleven

AROUND THE TIME I was experimenting with the new antide-pressant, I started having conflicts with my softball teammates. Larry faithfully attended all of my Tuesday evenings games. The early games at six p.m. were great, but the nine o'clock games were brutal. For the late games, I dragged my sons out on a school night, bribing them with candy and ice cream. Or I left them at home (they were old enough at this point) and spent the evening full of worry, hoping they wouldn't let anyone inside and they'd do their homework. I was the only person on the team with children who showed up every week, without fail. If we were short a female player, I got the panicked call to help find someone to fill the roster. I'd learned to keep an ear out at my sons' school for moms or dads who played softball.

But for all my dependability, what did I get, benched. As the season wore on, I found myself sitting more often. It made me livid when one of the women took left-center field and stuck me at catcher when she couldn't run after a fly ball, literally. She'd injured her leg and could only hobble after balls. Despite her injury, she insisted on being out on the field. So, I'd sit on the bench or play catcher and resent the fact I'd left my kids at home to do god only knows what for this. When she came to the dugout after my second inning of sitting out, I said, "This is so unfair. I'm always sitting out when you can't even make the cutoff."

"Marie, I don't have time for this." She moved to the other end of the dugout and I sat there fuming, my heart pounding as I tried not to cry. The game finally ended with another loss. Our team, after several strong seasons in a lower-division, had gotten cocky and overly ambitious; we were now playing in an upper-division against teams that could easily out-hit and out-field us. We'd become a joke. By mid-game, teams would start telling their runners to slow it down, don't go crazy to get around the bases. Let's not rub their faces in it.

Gloomy with another loss, everyone gathered outside the dugout to decide on dinner plans. Larry stood off to the side holding my water bottle and glove. I knew there was no way I was having dinner with the gang and pretending that things were hunky-dory, and really, fuck them all. I let my bipolar fly.

"I'm so sick of being treated unfairly," I screamed so loud that I got everyone's attention immediately, even the umps'. "I thought the purpose was to have fun. Win or lose, that was supposed to be secondary. But now you get to decide who plays and who doesn't. I don't leave my kids at home so I can fucking sit on the bench. I don't mind sitting my fair share, but why is it I sit out half the game when others sit out, maybe, once a game?"

Larry stood off to the side, thinking, I was sure, *Holy shit! She's lost it.* I'd never gone completely off like this in front of him, but here I was making an ass of myself while my softball friends just looked disgusted and annoyed. One man tried to interrupt me, tried to say something reasonable to help me calm down, but I screamed over him until my voice was hoarse. I grabbed my equipment and stormed off. We drove home in silence. I was mortified by my behavior and too ashamed to even apologize for humiliating him.

The next Sunday, I went out for our weekly pickup game and saw my teammates. I apologized to a few of them. The man who had tried to talk me off the ledge at Tuesday's game said, "So did you and Larry break up?"

"No, why?"

"Well, I figured after he saw you lose it, he'd hit the road. You were kind of scary."

"I was furious and hurt. I think he knew it had been building up."

"Yeah, well, you might have lucked out with him. I think most guys would have hit the road."

His words had spoken to my greatest fear—that I was basically unlovable, especially from a man's point of view. A successful, unflawed man, a man worthy of an attractive, successful, smart, and mentally stable woman wouldn't give me a moment's notice. I was lucky to have Larry, I told myself. Even with all of his shortcomings, he stuck it out. I told myself that I should count every moment he stood beside me as a blessing. I had let my crazy fly, and he was still there to console me.

chapter twelve

YEARS BEFORE MEETING Larry, my parents had died and left me a trust fund. For a decade or so, my account grew and grew. It seemed that making money in the stock market was a no-brainer. However, as the 2008 financial crisis came into view, my stocks started behaving like children on crack: one month they'd be flying high, up ninety to one hundred and twenty thousand dollars, and then the next month, they'd crash with a seventy or eighty-thousand-dollar hangover. It wouldn't be long before the stock market crash eliminated fifty percent of my portfolio and wiped out forty percent of the estimated value of my house.

I was in the middle of self-publishing my second memoir and not earning a salary. Each month I transferred at least fifteen thousand dollars from the rapidly diminishing principal balance of my trust for my sons and me to live on. I was constantly worried about running out of money. One night at dinner—a beautiful, fresh slab of salmon with steaming vegetables and rice pilaf, I was listening to my sons whine about being forced to eat salmon.

"Do you know how much this fish cost?" I asked. They shook their heads while Larry started serving himself. "Twenty-five dollars."

"We didn't ask you to buy it," my older son Austin said so matter-of-fact. "You know we don't like it."

"Yeah, mom," Zack chimed. "We never like it."

"Well, it's good for you and you need to eat some. Squeeze some lemon on it."

The conversation became a familiar monologue about my panic over money. I complained about the twelve to fourteen thousand dollars I was spending a month, the cost of Austin's private school tuition (a school he hated and didn't want to attend), their BMX bikes, our housekeeper, the publishing and marketing expenses for my new memoir, this and that until their eyes had glossed over and they began picking at the fish. I knew they were too young to burden them with these worries. I, not my sons, had created our precarious financial situation. If I'd had greater self-control and were a better parent, I would have kept these worries and the blaming to myself.

Larry generally stayed out of our family disagreements, but suddenly he held his fork aloft. "I don't know why you spend so much money. I live comfortably on twelve hundred dollars a month."

I looked at him and wanted to fling a forkful of rice pilaf at him. *What are you talking about?* Even if my sons and I cut out movies, dinners out, vacations, and even if we gave up our housekeeper, traded private school for public, and I didn't spend another penny on my publishing business, we'd still never survive on twelve hundred a month. Our mortgage alone was three times that. Health insurance, another fourteen hundred.

Larry had recently moved from the rented bedroom in Oakland to a friend's ranch house in Pleasant Hill. The friend had inherited the house from her deceased parents and was charging Larry nominal rent for his handyman services. He would fix up the house, including ridding the bedrooms of urine-soaked carpets and cigarette-stained drywall. He didn't have the expense of private health insurance, whether it was truly unaffordable because his history of cancer or if he felt that a free county hospital was sufficient. He seemed to believe if it ain't broke, don't fix it. Why spend money on a dentist or eye doctor unless your crusty teeth or eyeballs start falling out? Income taxes? That's for idiots who actually declare their income. And food, why buy it and cook it yourself if you can get your girlfriend and friends to feed you?

"Yes." I sighed. "Well, good for you."

The next morning at breakfast, after Larry left for his handyman job, I explained to my sons that Larry was a world-class mooch and that no family in the San Francisco Bay Area could live reasonably well on twelve hundred dollars a month.

"Have you noticed how he never pays for meals when we go out?" I asked as they ate their three dollars a serving sugary cereal. "Have you ever seen him bring over dinner or even dessert?"

Not that I wanted to make Larry look bad in front of my sons, but I was defensive after Austin had accused me of having a spending problem. And I'd felt like such a lousy parent after Zack had recently asked, "Mom, are we really going to have to sell our house and move?"

"You can afford to live like a miser when you're constantly fed by your girlfriend, or Jane, or ex-in-laws, or your friends," I said, recycling a complaint that my friends had heard many times. "Or if you're willing to live in a stinky house." As they readied for school, I wondered how Larry could be so lackadaisical about his future or retirement. I constantly worried about mine. I often dreamed of my parents coming back to life, asking me to return my inheritance, and me having to admit that I'd carelessly spent it all, and we had nothing left. Larry had had cancer, and sure he was past the seven-year survival rate, but he couldn't be certain it wouldn't return. How did he know that he wouldn't need a financial safety net if he got sick or fell off a ladder or electrocuted himself with his shoddy electrical work? He had problems with his ankles. Supposedly, that was why he gave up playing volleyball. How much longer could a fifty-five-year-old man crawl around attics or dig trenches or haul lumber?

After building my pool and helping me with a few other small projects, Larry returned to doing handyman jobs for Jane. She had sold her engineering business and had now started flipping houses, in earnest, with one of their volleyball friends. It baffled me that she'd hired Larry to do anything more complicated than hanging sheetrock. She knew I had had to pay my regular handyman to fix Larry's shoddy wiring work. That I'd hired him to hang a series of five plates above the slider in my kitchen and watched him struggle for an hour to calculate the spacing so that the plates hung an equal distance apart and centered over the door. When she told me that she put him in charge of the electrical work in her spec houses, I laughed and said, "I hope you've got good insurance."

I knew Larry could be bought. There was an air of entitlement about him. It made me envious that he always seemed to get a free ride. A *free ride*, I knew, wasn't quite accurate. His mom had died when he was a teenager. He and his brother had ended up in foster care, but they'd been well-cared for by their foster parents. His father was basically a no-show. I wasn't sure if the man had died; I'd never really asked much about him. But Larry had friends, an ex-wife, and even ex-in-laws who kept thinking up work to keep him afloat. Family and friends who always had birthday and Christmas gifts and meals to share with him. Everyone loved Larry. Larry wouldn't hurt a fly, and he was always there to help. As my financial situation worsened, I realized that I had been buying his companionship, and yet the payoff (having a man to share my bed, a movie partner, a fourth person at the table) didn't offset the cost. Resentment built as I understood that I'd compromised on what I now really wanted in a relationship—someone as equally ambitious, creative, intellectually curious, and self-sufficient as I was (or hoped to be once the economy rebounded). Someone who didn't just rely on others to provide for him. Someone curious enough about me to read my published and soon-to-be-published memoirs.

After mailing out fifteen hundred advance reader copies of my second memoir and purchasing booths at various book events, I scheduled book signings in Lafayette, Baton Rouge, New Orleans, and other areas of Louisiana. I bribed Larry with free food, hotel, and airfare to come along as my literary assistant. All around the San Francisco Bay Area, he'd been helping me get from Point A to Point B. On this trip, he would meet some of my six sisters, who thought he was nice, maybe a little *too* nice for me. It was a stressful week: a lot of driving back and forth across the Lake Pontchartrain Causeway. A lot of empty bookstores. A lot of self-doubts and financial worry. During a major financial crisis, had I just pissed away a hundred thousand dollars (or more) on publishing and marketing these books? Had I squandered money I needed to support my kids and myself and later my retirement?

We crisscrossed South Louisiana, sometimes driving for hours without conversation. I realized after a couple of nights, neither of us had made an overture for sex. In fact, we'd barely touched or kissed. A few months earlier, I'd told him I loved him, and then after the initial excitement of making that proclamation wore off and he'd bashfully professed his love for me, I quit saying it. I cared about him. Sure. But love, love was over-reaching, an obvious exaggeration. For a while, he continued to tell me he loved me, but eventually, without my reciprocation, he stopped. So now we hauled around books and luggage for a week. We exchanged a quick kiss goodnight, but the subject of sex never came up. Later, I would wonder if he was grateful for the reprieve.

Approaching Baton Rouge, I was driving and Larry was white-knuckling the door handle, shooting me frightened looks as I swerved in and out of traffic to outmaneuver the idiots who were getting in the way of my making it on time to my next reading. Larry cleared his throat, and in a stern voice, one I'd never heard him use before, he said, "Slow down before you kill us. We're not going to get there any faster if you drive like a manic."

I turned to him and hissed, "Yeah, well, your breath stinks!" I froze and thought, *did I really just tell him that his breath stinks? Yes. Ugh.* Words that had been flitting around my mind for months had flown right out of my mouth like spears. *Marie, you're a cruel bitch sometimes.* I couldn't look at him. I was so ashamed. His breath really stank. I had wanted to say so forever, but I'd never imagined that I'd do so minutes before we were to pull into the Barnes & Noble parking lot for a book event. Sometimes I had no idea why he put up with me.

We silently walked to the entrance. He held open the door, and I mumbled, "Thanks." As I found my way to the customer service desk to ask for the store manager, Larry went to find the novel he'd started reading days earlier in the first book store. Rather than purchase the popular paperback, he simply remembered the page he'd left off and re-shelved it. At the next event, while I spoke or signed books or tried not to look desperate and bored sitting by myself behind a table stacked with my books, he'd go off in the corner and read another fifty or hundred pages of the novel until, as our tour came to an end, he finished it. In this way, he was very self-sufficient—an underrated quality in a boyfriend, and I liked that about him. He never whined, "I'm bored. How much longer?" When a book store manager flirted with me and offered to buy me dinner, Larry just stood there looking indifferent, and later in the car, we laughed about it.

New Orleans was the last stop of the trip. On the evening before flying back to San Francisco, we ate an early dinner, content to simply people-watch instead of making conversation. We looked like one of those old, tired couples you see in restaurants whose only exchanged words were with the server. At least we weren't nose-down in our cell phones.

On the way back to our hotel, walking through the French Quarter, I noticed two women sitting at a table in the dimly lit doorway of a closed antique shop. They had transformed a few square feet of dirty cement into a living room: a worn armchair, floral skirted table, a vintage rug, candles, and a kitchen chair. I tugged on Larry's sleeve and stopped to watch. Tarot cards were spread out on the table. I loved having my cards read. Sometimes the readings were eerily spot-on, and other times, the readers were simply con artists, obviously relying on cues from my body language or making ridiculous predictions based on my appearance and apparent age or telling me what they thought I wanted to hear. I'd spent a decade waiting to meet my future husband, a wealthy Middle Eastern merchant, as foretold by a psychic, only to accept finally that she was a con and I'd been swindled out of forty dollars.

This middle-aged hippie looked legitimate, because really, who would go to all the trouble to haul their living room to the French Quarter in the middle of January and huddle in a doorway with strangers if they didn't truly believe they had a gift that must be shared with others? Certainly, there were easier ways to make money—even in a recession. While Larry shifted from foot to foot, yawning every couple of seconds, I kept staring at the reader so that when she noticed me, I could point to myself and mouth, "I'm next, please."

"Ready," Larry asked after I'd been watching for a couple of minutes.

"No, I want to have her read my cards."

"I'm exhausted," he said. "I just want to go back to our room and get off my feet."

"It won't take long," I pleaded. "I'll pay for yours as well."

"Not interested. I'm cold." He sighed, but I didn't budge. If I moved from our spot, I was afraid another customer would take my place in line.

"Please." I took his hand and warmed it in mine. "I promise we'll go straight to the hotel after." I still felt guilty about telling him that his breath stank earlier in the week, and as a penance, I should have relented. But I really wanted to ask someone who might have divine powers to give me financial and career advice. While we waited, it occurred to me I wasn't carrying much cash in my purse and I might not have enough money. A few years earlier, I'd been part of a tour group held up at gunpoint in the Garden District, and now when I visited New Orleans, I carried only a small amount of cash, my California driver's license, and one credit card outside of the hotel. I looked for a sign stating the fee. I doubted she accepted credit cards, although that would have been convenient. I thought about asking Larry how much cash he had on him, but figured that might really perturb him, and he'd head back to the hotel.

When it was my turn, I sat down and asked, "What's your fee?"

"I don't charge my clients." She picked up her worn deck of tarot cards. "If you'd like to make a donation, I would be happy to accept sixty dollars."

"Oh. I only have forty. Would you accept that?" Tarot card readers and psychics must hate the low-balling and haggling. She nodded and reached down on the floor beside her armchair and set a lacquered box on the table. I was told to put my money in the box and then we'd begin.

"While you shuffle the deck seven times, think about what you most want to know," the woman instructed as I sat on the edge of the chair. "Don't tell me your question. Just focus your energy as it passes to the cards."

Questions swirled around my mind: *Would I ever be a successful writer? Should I go back to accounting? Am I going to run out of money? Were my kids emotionally scarred by the divorce and all the conflicts between their father and me? Was it selfish to write about my life, and in doing so, exposing my family? Would I ever be free of depression? Should I break up with Larry?* I couldn't actually ask the last question since he was standing nearby.

I cut the deck and set the two stacks face down. Next, she merged the stacks and fanned out the cards. "Select seven cards," she said, and then laid the seven cards I selected out in some meaningful order. "What is your question?"

"Will I have to sell my house?" I asked, surprising myself. It hadn't been one of the questions I'd considered, but it catapulted its way into my consciousness. I pictured our house on Freeman Road, the house my sons and I utterly adored. I had spent a decade renovating it room by room. A handmade beveled glass front door that I'd painted fire engine red. The Bill Huebbe monkey chandelier in the dining room. The massive walk-in master closet with cedar floors that Zack told his teacher was bigger than his bedroom (not entirely true). The wall-to-wall windows in the living room that overlooked fruit trees and lilacs. Lynne's hand-carved and painted tiles around the fireplace and in the kitchen. My beautiful rose garden that my softball friends, led by April, had planted, and I'd nurtured. Even the ridiculous above-ground swimming pool that Larry had miraculously completed the installation. Our nearly half-acre backyard where my sons and their friends had created dirt jumps and ramps for their bikes and skate-boards. I'd hosted parties and game nights galore over the years. It was a well-loved house in a neighborhood that felt safe and neighborly.

I waited for the tarot reader to tell me whether I'd put myself in such a financial bind with my publishing business and exorbitant spending that I must now sell my house. It was the question that kept me up at night. The question I asked myself when I was alone and cried softly into my pillow so my sons wouldn't hear me. I knew I hadn't simply *found* myself in this situation. I'd created this situation where I might be faced with selling my house in a down market. I felt like a total failure. I'd gone through most of my inheritance. I knew there were millions of people who had it much worse. At least my house wasn't underwater. We could probably find something cheaper, but finding a more affordable house would likely mean moving to another city, changing schools, leaving their friends, all because I had been so selfish and foolish.

She didn't give me a straight yes or no. Rather, she said that I'd sunk a lot of money into my house. It held a lot of good memories and reflected who I was as a person and artist. But it had also become a money pit, something I could no longer afford. She could see I was carrying a lot of stress over this decision. She saw my sons and me living somewhere else. There might be an interim house, but we'd definitely end up in another home. It wasn't what I'd hoped to hear, but it wasn't unexpected. I'd wanted to hear that my financial setback was only temporary, that a big windfall was just around the corner. But she told me these truths: I could no longer afford the house. I needed to get a job (the same thing the family court judge had ordered me to do a month earlier), most likely go back to accounting, continue to write on the side, but definitely, sell my house.

chapter thirteen

I TOOK UP springboard diving at age thirty-six when my sons were learning to swim at a school in Lafayette, California. I started with private lessons and within a few weeks had learned dives in each of the five categories, thus earning me a spot on the team. Except for a few master divers, the team consisted mainly of kids ranging in ages from seven to eighteen. At practices, I often found myself diving with my sons' classmates or peers.

I invited Larry to watch one of my practices. As an easy-going, friendly guy, he immediately hit it off with my coach and fellow divers. He loyally began attending my dive practices. A lot of parents watched the practices, especially those with the younger children who couldn't yet drive themselves to and from practices, so it wasn't unusual for a grownup to hang around the pool deck. Twice a week, Larry would sit next to my coach under the red umbrella and cheer on my teammates and me as we went through our lists on the one- and three-meter boards. He was always ready with a big bear hug for some more affectionate pre-teen and teenage girls who knew him as Marie's friendly boyfriend.

Questions I Should Have Asked, #17: Was it strange that my boyfriend was so chummy with these young girls?

In January 2009, as the high school dive season approached, the schools were scrambling to find a diving coach. As often happened, they'd released the previous coach without a backup plan or an explanation. I was busy with the upcoming release of my second memoir and was half-heartedly updating my resume, knowing that I should start looking for a job. Urged on by the parents at our club, however, I applied for the head coach job and was hired by the district to coach their four high schools. Although I'd been diving for nine years and the master divers and I often coached each other during practices, I hadn't a clue how to run varsity and junior varsity dive teams. Many of the varsity divers would be performing dives that I'd never executed—a reverse one and a half, for instance. There was no way I could demonstrate one. Could I command their confidence and respect? I worried about kids hurting themselves during my watch and about being sued along with the school district. To prepare myself and avoid looking like a fool, I bought and borrowed coaching manuals and DVDs. I spent hours watching YouTube instructional videos of nationally recognized coaches. I sought advice from my coaches and others in our area. I also figured I'd rely on the diving progressions, drills, modeling, and stretches that I'd learned when first starting out.

Besides doubting my expertise, I worried about false accusations. I had learned the reason for the prior coach's abrupt and humiliating dismissal: he'd reposted a silly meme on Facebook that parents thought was inappropriate. I worried about parents combing through my social media accounts or reading my memoirs and taking offense by something I've said or done. What if, in demonstrating a correct movement or proper form, a child misinterpreted my touching as something other than professional? My own dive coaches were great role models. I'd never witnessed or heard any rumors of impropriety. But I wondered, what if an athlete, for whatever reason, decided he or she didn't like me and wanted to make my life hell? Having been around teenagers, I knew they often traded speculation and rumors about teachers and coaches as if they were verifiable facts. In high school, many of my classmates and I thought nothing of secretly maligning a priest for being a little too friendly or youthfully hand-some. Would I become one of these adults whose reputation the kids smeared just for the fun of gossiping or to shift the spotlight away from themselves? I didn't want to become one of those poor saps dra-matized in movies and novels who are falsely accused of inappropriate behavior and suddenly faced with lawsuits and financial ruin.

I knew that the affluent, well-educated parents in our community demanded a lot from their children's teachers and coaches. I'd coached my sons' soccer teams and led a Cub Scouts troop, and the parents, and even some children, could be intimidating as hell. There were times, admittedly, that I'd been demanding and impatient with my sons' coaches and teachers. There was the issue of dealing with four school administrations. Dual meets to schedule, rules to learn, equip-ment to manage. The knowledge my sons were embarrassed to have me on campus. Coaching three levels of divers—Future Champions (novices invited to try out the sport to help build the teams), JV, and Varsity—at four different schools meant recruiting for and managing four schools, miles apart from each other, coaching and coordinating four sets of divers of varying abilities.

Rather than obsess about all the what-ifs, I focused on the incred-ible opportunity to share my passion for dive with these enthusiastic students. I'd get to know my sons' classmates and school adminis-trations better. I loved being around teenagers. Having sons, I was constantly driving around a car full of smelly and loud teenage boys. I loved their energy and enthusiasm. The fact they thought they were so wise, and yet they were still so naïve. I loved seeing their struggle to figure out where and how they fit in. I loved their banter. I loved that they were idealistic, flawed, confused, tender, self-assured, insecure, tough, shy, bold, silly, serious. I loved how they sought me out for advice, shared their concerns and successes. I'd arrive at my club dive practice and hear one of the kids shout my name, rush over to tell me he or she had just thrown a new dive. I loved that my praise mattered to them.

Knowing that I was apprehensive about coaching, Larry, who had coached middle school girls' volleyball, began giving me advice on what to do and expect. The dos and don'ts of managing a team.

Questions I Should Have Asked, #18: If you could undo one mistake in your years of coaching, what would that be?

The night before my first practice, we went out for pizza. As I locked the front door, Larry looked at my tennis shoes. "You need to buy better shoes. You want to look like a real coach." I looked at my scuffed tennis shoes. There were no holes. The laces weren't frayed or missing. They had at least another six months of life.

"Who's going to notice my shoes?" I asked. *Other than my sons,* I thought. It annoyed them that I bought the most marked-down tennis shoes I could find rather than the trendiest, expensive brands. "Why does it even matter? I know most of the divers and their parents," I said as I walked to the car. There was something silly and misplaced about his concern over my footwear. It reminded me of that scene in *Ordinary People,* where Beth tells Conrad to wear different socks for their son's funeral.

"It doesn't look very professional," Larry said. "You want to make a good impression, don't you?"

Making a good first impression was important. I wanted to look the part of the professional coach. However, replaying these words in my mind, now years later, I'm struck by how odd it was that he spent three years in jail for molestation and statutory rape, and yet his most pressing advice was regarding my choice of footwear.

chapter fourteen

THE TWO THOUSAND DOLLARS dive coaching stipend would be a great end-of-the-season bonus when it arrived in June, but it wouldn't pay even a month's mortgage. After Larry and I returned from New Orleans and the dive season got underway, I kept thinking about my tarot card reading. The woman—whether she was genuine or a fraud—had been right. I was constantly worrying about my finances and regretting all the money I'd sunk into my house. I'd refinanced the mortgage numerous times, each time taking out money for more improvements, vacations, tuition, and a livelihood while I wrote full time. Even though the current equity was far less than when I purchased the house, it was my biggest asset after I'd nearly depleted my savings.

I woke up one morning to find that the constant buzzing and whirling in my head had stopped. I had realized in the middle of the night that it was self-defeating to keep second-guessing myself, flip-flopping between hopeless and hopelessness, feeling ashamed and scared. I dropped my sons off at their respective schools and felt the exquisite absence of panic. It had been at least two years since my head felt this clear, my mind this calm. I was finally resigned to accepting that whatever happened next, I'd deal with it. With a mug of tea, I sat at my computer and looked around my office. Three of the four walls were floor-to-ceiling windows and sliding glass doors facing my side, front, and back yards. There was greenery visible from every pane of glass—hundred-year-old oaks, lilacs, cherry trees. My prized persimmon tree that my mailman sometimes parked beside and stood on the roof of his truck to pick the fruit from the highest branches. I smiled proudly at the small dining patio I'd created by laying large slabs of flagstone off the kitchen slider and then boxed in for privacy with fast-growing privet hedges.

Feeling grounded and optimistic, I turned on my computer and began creating Excel spreadsheets. I looked at our finances under different scenarios, but the bottom line was always the same. We couldn't afford the house anymore since I had used it as an ATM. Though this was an incredibly sad reality to face, and I couldn't fault anyone but myself, I told myself to have faith that one day we would own another property. We wouldn't be renting forever. We'd find another home, maybe not one we loved as much, but one that met our needs.

Larry came for dinner that evening. I hadn't said anything to Austin or Zack after school because I'd over shared too many of my financial concerns already and they were too young to help carry this burden. After they went to sleep, Larry and I climbed into my bed. Before I opened my newspaper, I whispered, "I've scheduled a few meetings with realtors. I'm going to get my house ready to sell by April."

"Wow. That was fast." He picked his thumbnail and asked, "You okay?"

I shrugged. "A mixture of sad, numb, angry, and panicked. But more than anything, I'm relieved. It's as if a tremendous burden has been lifted just by making a decision."

"What will you do after it sells? Would you move back to Louisiana?"

"No, I can't do that. The kids wouldn't want to leave their friends and school, and I don't think their dad would allow it." A thought occurred to me, and impulsively, I asked, "What would you say to the guys and me moving in with you? Be honest. You can say no. I'll completely understand, but you've got three bedrooms and extra space. Maybe we could move in for a few months to save money and look for a new house."

"Sure," Larry said.

"Really?" I smiled. "You don't want to think about it?"

He shook his head. He looked genuinely happy.

"You realize that means Toby and Shelby would come along as well? You don't mind our cats?"

"It will be fun. I like the idea. Guess I'll have to get around to replacing the carpets and drywall in the old cat room."

"Yes, please. The kids would die if they had to live with that odor." Austin and Zack would not be happy when they saw the house; this I also knew. They would be less thrilled with the Pleasant Hill neighborhood—its proximity to the freeway and distance from their friends and schools. If their father suddenly decided to move out of our current school district, forcing my sons to attend school in Larry's district, we'd be screwed. But there was no sense worrying about that now. It's just a temporary move, I told myself. My sons would see how less affluent people lived. They'd get to know kids who didn't drive, nor expect to drive, Mercedes, Lexuses, or twelve hundred-dollar bikes to school. It would be character building. A few months, maybe even a year. Plus, it really might be fun.

Larry left early the next morning to make plans for replacing the damaged flooring and drywall. Normally, he'd fix a pot of coffee and leave the French press in the sink for me to clean, but he was in a hurry to get home and start working on the cat room.

Questions I Should Have Asked, #19: Are you rushing out of my house this morning to hide or destroy anything untoward?

As I dropped off Austin at his school and headed to drop off Zack, I thought about how readily Larry had agreed to let us move into his house. With Mike, the first time I left my toothbrush at his house, I found it placed next to my purse as a hint to take it home. If the roles were reversed and Larry had asked to move in with me and my sons, I would have needed a lot more time to consider the implications to our household. I wondered if he ever secretly drank. Were there empty bottles in his garbage can at this very moment? Would my sons and I find ourselves living with an on-and-off drunk? That would be a hard-stop for me.

I suddenly realized that for all the time Larry and I had spent together, nearly thirteen months, I didn't truly know him. He was okay as a boyfriend, as long as I didn't expect much. But his standard of living and laziness were two things I couldn't tolerate day in and day out, and living with him, that would be unavoidable. The French coffee press was a perfect example of his laziness. Every time he left the dirty coffee maker in my sink, and I took it apart, soaped and rinsed away the annoying coffee grinds stuck to the filter, plate, and beaker, I fumed that he was so presumptuous and lazy. He had to have known it wouldn't miraculously clean itself and find its way back to the cabinet every day. A few weeks back, I had watched him set the dirty press in the sink, and I waited to see if he'd clean it. I didn't say a word until he picked up his mug of hot coffee and started to leave the kitchen.

"You aren't going to wash that?"

"What? Oh, I hate washing it. It's a pain in the butt."

"Do you think that I like washing it any more than you do? And I don't even drink coffee." He laughed as if to brush me off as petty or silly. I was sure his thoughts went something like: "Oh, come on. You're going to wash a ton of dishes and pots throughout the day and evening anyway. What's one more item?"

Would a responsible parent move her sons in with a guy she had serious misgivings about? I wondered. Had I given this impulsive decision enough consideration?

On a whim, I took a different route driving home after dropping the boys off at school. I turned onto Jane's street and saw a "For Lease" sign in her neighbor's yard. My heart started beating rapidly. In a state of euphoria, I stared at that "For Lease" sign. I pulled my car to the curb and looked at the yellow rancher with tremendous gratitude. This rental house with its teal blue door and squat green hedges might as well have been a neon marquee flashing: *For Christ's sake, woman! Don't move in with Larry.*

"Thank you, thank you, thank you." I reached into my purse for my cell phone. As I dialed the realtor's number, I let out an enormous sigh. I felt giddy as I introduced myself. I was dizzy with excitement and disbelief, knowing I'd stumbled upon something that was exactly what I needed at that moment—even if I hadn't realized it until right then. This yellow rancher was a sign—a gift from the universe. A feeling was percolating in my gut, nudging me to make better decisions.

Sometimes, in my *Oh, poor me* moods, I'd swear that the only luck I knew intimately was bad luck. I had finished both undergraduate and graduate schools only to face economies where finding a well-paying job in my career seemed as likely as George Clooney calling to ask me to be his next leading lady. I'd applied for dozens of entry-level banking jobs in the San Francisco Financial District and secured not even one interview. Instead, I ended up taking a bookkeeping job at Fisherman's Wharf. Memoirs were all the rage, of course, until I started shopping one around. The guys I absolutely adored, the ones that all the girls vied for—Todd, Johnny, Bubba, Shelly, Perry, Marshall, Jack—I couldn't nab.

My luck just sucked.

Until it didn't.

As I've gotten older and hopefully wiser, I've realized that sometimes good luck comes in the form of near misses. I've thought about all the times in high school and college, after Jungle Juice and keg parties, I drove totally blotto and never killed anyone, including myself. Surely that was luck or good fortune riding shotgun. I'd hitchhiked twice without incident. Another time, another place, there might have been other drivers on these same roads who would have come upon me—a stranded young, defenseless, trusting woman, and who would have stopped to give me a lift but not deliver me to my desired destination. Maybe that time I traveled to Mexico alone, took an open bottle of champagne to my hotel room (the bottle the bartender had insisted on opening even though I'd argued against), which had been, unbeknownst to me, laced with drugs. Maybe I was lucky that I passed out after only one glass so that when the bartender and his friend jimmied the lock on the sliding glass door, I managed through the fog of the drugs to mumble, however incoherently, that they get out or I'd scream—one more glass and maybe . . . well, who knows.

Perhaps the Dalai Lama was right when he said, "Remember that sometimes not getting what you want is a wonderful stroke of luck." Who knew how my life would have turned out had I nabbed any of the Todds, Dougs, Bubbas, Mikes, Johnnys, Shellys, Perrys, Marshalls, Jacks . . . I so badly wanted? I truly believed I had been blessed not to be forced to reckon with what I thought I so terribly wanted or needed and blessed that I had survived near misses that I wasn't even aware of.

From the outside, the yellow rental house appeared to be in nice condition. The two-car garage had been converted into a studio or extra bedroom, which would become a hotly contested space between my sons and me. Best of all, it was in the same school district my sons attended. My sons could hang out with Jane's son. They'd still be able to ride their bikes to their dad's and friends' houses. And Jane and I could visit and have tea anytime. Parked at the curb, I called the agent and inquired about leasing the house. As I drove off with a flyer, I thought about how in twelve hours, I'd gone from asking Larry if we could move into his house to deciding my sons and I should instead rent this house. It was difficult to know whether I was having a bipolar episode or behaving rationally. But this seemed like a stroke of luck: finding an affordable rental house in our neighborhood next to one of my best friends.

As I completed the application, I thought about Larry's reaction later when I'd tell him the news. I knew he'd be disappointed and confused. I met the realtor an hour later and we toured the house, the large yard and deck, and the in-law unit off the driveway. By noon, I'd turned in my application, given her first and last months' rent plus a security deposit.

Larry joined us for dinner that evening. He'd begun tearing out the carpet and baseboards from the cat room, he announced. I shook my head discretely. For a moment, he seemed baffled by my reaction, but then his face seemed to register an understanding that I either hadn't said anything to my sons or I had and it wasn't well-received, so please, for now, don't say anything further on the subject. I whispered, "Sorry, we'll talk later," yet dreading the conversation we'd have. But then again, I rationalized, the carpet needed replacing, and this was simply giving him the nudge he needed to start the work.

After we climbed into bed and buried ourselves under two goose down comforters, I said, "I'm really sorry to do this, but the boys and I won't be moving in with you. I found a rental house right next to Jane's. We're taking possession on the first of April."

"But I'm confused." He picked his nail. "When did this come about? You just invited yourself and the boys to live with me."

"I changed my mind." I cringed with guilt. He hadn't truly been part of a family since his divorce. And before that, he'd lived in foster care after his mom died. I felt as if I'd dangled a family right in front of his face, only to snatch it away when he reached for it. "I need to start making smart financial and lifestyle changes, starting with selling my house," I said.

"Lifestyle changes?"

"Yep. I'm going to get a job and put my house on the market. I'm going to let our housekeeper go and start teaching the boys to do laundry and clean up after ourselves. No more money on my publishing business until I start generating a profit. No more baseball fantasy camps, Club Med vacations, extravagant dinners, or birthday parties. We're going to learn to live within our means."

He didn't say anything. He just stared blankly ahead at the pocket doors that lead to the master bath.

"Are you disappointed," I asked. He shrugged. *Well, that makes it easier if you're so indifferent.* "I'm sorry that I changed my plans so quickly. I just think we're not ready to live together."

He nodded and yawned. I leaned back from the smell of decay on his breath. He really needed to see a dentist.

chapter fifteen

IN APRIL, MY SONS and I moved out of our Freeman Street house into the rental. We had left much of the furnishings and artwork behind to stage the house. I was now paying rent and upkeep on the rental plus the mortgage and upkeep on our house. It was important that my house sell quickly, leaving no money on the table. On the eve of the broker's open, the Freeman house was pristine and ready for viewing. I'd swept the driveway and sidewalk. I'd dead-headed the roses and pulled weeds. The grime had been scraped from the hard-to-reach crevices in the kitchen floor boards, and pillows fluffed, fruit bowls arranged to look perfect but natural, every wall and surface checked for handprints or smudges of dirt, the cluttered garage straightened—all the important details to help bring in competing full-price or above-asking offers. After twelve hours of gardening and cleaning, the last thing I wanted to do was bake a German chocolate cake for Larry's birthday. Yet, out of guilt, I'd baked his favorite cake. After all, he'd taken my decision not to move in with him fairly well. He never brought up the subject again.

He arrived for his celebratory dinner at our new rental. I hadn't given him a key yet, so when the doorbell rang, I called out to Zack to please let Larry in as I had four burners going.

"Happy birthday." I kissed and hugged Larry. Zack leaned against the refrigerator and Larry stood next to me at the sink. Three people were the maximum the small kitchen could comfortably accommodate. "Dinner is just about ready." Before he could launch into a minute-by-minute recap of his day, I cut him off, saying, "I made a cake for your birthday."

He lifted the plastic dome and saw the sugary coconut frosting. I watched him lick his lips and rub his belly while making that annoying *mmmm* sound he made over food. Zack looked utterly disappointed when he saw the frosting. He might pick around the gooey topping, but Austin wouldn't even try the cake.

"Happy birthday," Zack said.

"How is your birthday going so far," I asked. Instead of launching into the painful details of whatever project he was working on, he said, "Great. I found Spam on sale at Safeway. I bought two cases!"

Zack's eyebrows shot up and we exchanged a horrified look. Admittedly, I ate Spam when I was younger, just as I ate Vienna sausages, Maraschino cherries, canned tamales, fried pork rinds, and other gross food items. But really, we lived in the San Francisco Bay Area and were surrounded with delicious, fresh food. What grownup, outside of Hawaii, who had so many better options, opted for a brick-shaped salty canned meat? The thought of the gelatinous pink meat sizzling in a frying pan and Larry licking his lips in anticipation of his first bite made me want to punch him in the throat. These would be the same lips that I might kiss. Ew.

At dinner, Larry asked how the guys liked the new house. Inwardly, I cringed. They were still angry at me for all the poor decisions that had led us to rent the house that had none of the conveniences that made their lives bearable, such as an ice maker and garbage disposal. They both shrugged.

"Admit it, Zack," I said, trying to lighten the mood with some gentle teasing. "You love your maroon carpeting and sharing a bathroom with mom." I pointed to Austin and said, "You came out the best in this whole deal. How many of your classmates have their own garage apartment with a refrigerator and private bathroom?"

Neither of them responded. They simply attacked their mashed potatoes, leaving the salmon and vegetables for last. When Larry left after dinner with three-quarters of the cake, Zack came into my bedroom and asked, "Mom, does Larry really eat Spam?"

I rolled my eyes and set down my newspaper. The bar I had set in accepting Larry as my boyfriend had fallen so low it was now laying on the ground. "Yes. I'm actually dating a man who eats Spam." I laughed although it wasn't funny. Sure, if I was stranded on a remote island and the only food available was Spam dropped by a helicopter, I'd gratefully pop open a can. No hesitation what so ever. But Larry wasn't starving. He wasn't stranded on an island. He wasn't broke. Even on a twelve hundred dollar a month budget, he didn't need to resort to canned meat. There was no way, I told myself, that I could continue to date a man who ate Spam. I might have sounded like a complete snob, but I had to draw the line somewhere. In retrospect, it is ironic that the impetus to break up with him was his affinity for Spam when in actuality, that was the least of his shortcomings.

chapter sixteen

THE FREEMAN HOUSE didn't sell as quickly as I'd hoped. The first offer I accepted fell out of escrow because the "pre-qualified" buyer couldn't get financing. We lowered the price based on the feedback we received from other agents. I'd given Larry's friend and her husband the listing at his recommendation and then had to fire them after a series of screw-ups. When I called the wife of the realtor couple to let her know I was relisting with a different agent now that our listing contract had expired, she screamed, "You have fucked me over. It's your fault the house isn't selling. I told you the price was too high. You're a perfect example of an unrealistic, greedy homeowner who refuses to listen to the expert they've hired."

She finally quit yelling and calmly said, "Okay. Let's start over. If you're unhappy with my husband, I can take him off the listing. I'll represent you alone." I covered the phone so she wouldn't hear me laughing. Her husband wasn't the problem. I couldn't believe she'd throw him under the bus without a speck of loyalty and then pretend that she hadn't just verbally assaulted me. I told her I was signing with another agent, her biggest rival, and she started yelling again. The funny thing was that a few weeks later, I was the guest author at her book club, and she was the perfect host. We both pretended that no harsh words or lost commission had ever come between us.

To tide us over financially while I kept up the two houses, I started selling the gold and silver coins I'd inherited from my parents. I sold a few to a softball friend who collected gold coins. My sons and I found a nearby coin show and filled Ziploc bags of coins to sell. After a typical, three-hundred-dollar grocery shopping trip, I decided Larry had to contribute. That evening, after dinner, Larry and I sat in the living room.

"We need to talk about a few things." I sat beside him on the sofa. "The guys and I love having you join us for dinner, but I can't afford all these groceries. I need you to chip in. Maybe you could buy groceries now and then, but no Spam, or give me some money toward the bills."

"Sure, I can do that," he said. I was so embarrassed to be having this conversation about money. Ashamed of him for not offering before, and ashamed for myself that I was in a position of having to ask for help. "And since Graciela isn't here anymore, I need you to help with the dishes."

He shook his head. "Then I'll just bring my own paper plates and plastic utensils."

"You're going to eat grilled salmon on a paper plate?" I sighed. *What an asshole.* "Anyway, we should start paying for our own movies, meals out, and entertainment."

He looked as if he'd been blindsided. He kept running his hand down his goatee and shifting on the cushion.

"One more thing," I whispered, so Zack couldn't hear me. "I've paid for the birth control this entire past year and it costs me about seventy-five dollars a month. Now it's your turn. Either you can reimburse me or wear a condom or get a vasectomy." He stared at me. I knew he didn't have health insurance, and I wasn't sure the county would pay for elective surgery. Of the three options, he agreed to pay for the birth control.

Several days before my birthday in May, I began seriously thinking about when to break up. After the Spam incident, it was simply a matter of timing. Despite being cheap about a lot of things, Larry was a generous gift-giver. I needed to take action soon. If we didn't break up before my birthday, then most likely he'd buy me something nice, like the Uggs he'd bought at Christmas, and I'd feel obliged to wait another few weeks.

On our typical Friday date night—dinner and a movie—we chose a cheap Mexican restaurant. When the server set the bill down and I saw the amount, twenty-six dollars, I expected him to say, "Hey, let me get this. This will be my treat." We had agreed to split everything down the middle, but as I watched him count out thirteen dollars plus three more for a tip, I thought, *this man has absolutely no pride if he's going to allow his girlfriend to pay for her thirteen-dollar dinner.*

"Do you mind if we stop at my house before the movie?" I said once we were seated in his truck.

"Sure. Everything okay?"

"Yeah."

We drove in silence. When we pulled up to the rental house, he parked. "Should I wait here?"

"No, why don't you come in."

My sons were at their father's house for the weekend. Toby and Shelby stood inside the door, waiting as we entered the living room. "We need to talk," I said. "Do you mind?" The cats followed us to the sofa and nudged Larry's arm. He was always good for a hearty neck scratch.

"I care a great deal about you," I began. He swallowed and looked down. I felt like such a bitch. "But I'm not happy. This isn't working anymore. I want to break up."

"I was worried this was going to happen." He shooed away the cats and picked his nails. "Would you change your mind if I helped with the dishes?"

"It's too late. I'm sorry." He nodded. "Do you want to stop over on Sunday to tell the boys? To say goodbye. I'm sure they'll miss you."

"Nah. They'll be fine."

That, more than anything, hurt. How could he not want to say goodbye to my sons? I figured, partly, it was to save face. No one liked to be dumped. Surely, he had cared for my sons. That had to have been real? Right?

We hugged and he left. Thirteen months—done. I locked the front door, poured a glass of water, and grabbed the newspaper to take to bed. Toby and Shelby followed me and jumped onto the comforter. My new bedroom was small, less than half the size of my previous one. The bookshelves were jammed together, covering every inch of wall space. I sat on my bed, an inflatable mattress, and as I petted the cats, I thought, *alone, once again.*

It was the strangest breakup I'd ever experienced. I never cried. If anything, I felt numb. I didn't have any regrets or temptation to call Larry to say I'd changed my mind or suggest we give it another go. I missed the familiarity of him. I missed having another adult at the dinner table. I missed sharing funny anecdotes about work and the boys. I missed having someone to read with in bed, to see movies, and to dine out. I missed the sex, even though he'd never overcome his inability to climax, but he was always accommodating.

Mostly, I didn't miss the resentful girlfriend I had become. The one who only half-listened when he shared his day with me, yet expected him to hang on my every word. From the beginning, I'd intentionally avoided falling for someone as hard as I had with Mike. It took five years of therapy, a daily regimen of antidepressants, shedding buckets of tears, writing thousands of angry pages, scaring my sons that I might injure myself, spending endless days moping and complaining to get over him. I never hoped or planned to go through that again. There was no way I'd love a man so intensely that I risked getting hurt again. Perhaps Larry had picked me for similar reasons.

Questions I Should Have Asked, #20: Why did you pick me? Was our relationship simply a cover for you?

I had set my expectations so low, and now I felt as if I was cheating myself out of the potential for real love.

chapter seventeen

BEFORE LARRY AND I broke up, he suggested I hire an attorney to renegotiate custody and child support. He felt my current support for two children was insufficient, especially since I was paying all of their expenses except for medical coverage. When their dad and I divorced, I only asked for a small amount of child support, figuring I had more assets and I wanted him to save to buy a house. Over the years, I had never asked for the support to be reevaluated. Now, money was tight. Also, I wanted more time with Austin and Zack. I felt short-changed in that their dad got to be the fun parent, and that except for holidays and summers, I got to be the parent telling them to do their home-work, get ready for school, and go to sleep. Their dad had remarried; he and his wife now had two young children. It seemed my sons were pushed aside and that rejection broke my heart. Tensions between our households increased over parenting styles—I was considered too lax. Yes, I had always allowed our house to be the hangout for my sons and their friends. It was important to me to monitor their activities and get to know their friends.

Through mediation, their father and I agreed on an 80/20 split, giving me primary custody. The next step was family court. I sat in a nearly packed court with my attorney for two hours, listening to unemployed, deadbeat parents beg the judge for leniency. When our case was called, my ex-husband stood and listed his complaints against me—the primary one that I'd humiliated him in his own community by writing and marketing two tell-all books. When he finished, I asked the judge if I could address his allegations. The judge adamantly refused. My request for additional child support based on the new custody agreement was denied. When I tried again to speak, he talked over me, saying I wasn't allowed to waste any more of the court's time. My attorney made no overture to speak on my behalf. The judge ordered me to pay half of all monthly medical costs going forward, and to get a job, ceasing, retroactively, all child support. My attorney, for her all ineptitude, cost me ten thousand dollars later in fees plus years of lost support.

Questions I Should Have Asked, #21: Why in the hell am I trusting Larry's legal and financial advice?

To abide by the court order (and avoid further interaction with this bastard judge, who I later learned treated other divorced moms the same way), I quickly sent out resumes and accepted the first of two job offers: office manager at an insurance agency. After my first day, I came home, thinking I'd made a huge mistake in choosing this job. (I had, in fact, arrived at the insurance office early that Monday morning to tell the agent I'd changed my mind and was rescinding my acceptance of his offer. But he'd been persuasive, and I allowed myself to be talked into staying on.)

"How was the new job?" Zack asked as I walked in after my first day and dropped my purse on the floor. "Not great," I answered. "Give me a few minutes and then I'll start dinner." I went into my office, put my head on my desk, and sobbed, thinking, *If I have to work at this job, or jobs like it for the next twenty to thirty years, I'd rather die right now. How in the fuck had it all come to this?*

A few months into working at the insurance agency, my Freeman house finally sold for sixty percent of what it had originally been listed for. For the next two years, we did our best to accept our new living situation, yet I constantly checked the real estate listings. Realtor after realtor told me that given my income and down payment, I couldn't afford to buy anything in the same school district. Just when I was about to renew my lease and admit that everyone was right—buying in the same area was hopeless—I saw that an unbelievably cheap fix-er-up house in my neighborhood had just been relisted on Redfin. The owner had died in the kitchen of natural causes, and the superstitious buyers backed out when this fact was disclosed. I couldn't believe my luck. Even though there was a sharp smell when I viewed the house, particularly in the kitchen (where the deceased had been found by her neighbor), and my sons complained, "Mom, we can see the highway signs from our bedroom windows and hear the traffic," I knew this was a great purchase. I may have poor judgment when it comes to men, but I've had about a ninety percent success rate with real estate. I took some money from both of my sons' college funds and combined it with what little remained in my trust to purchase the house.

The house was tiny and the closet space practically nil. Austin and Zack built a loft bed for me so I could use the bottom space as a closet. I just had to remember when climbing up the ladder to duck to avoid hitting my head on the exposed beam. Despite having given away or sold several pieces of furniture, knickknacks, art, hundreds of books, half of the remaining furniture and belongings still didn't fit inside the house. We crammed what we could inside the gardening shed and stuffed some in the musty storage space in the carport, and bought an additional storage unit for the side yard. Once the rains started and we saw that the disintegrating shed door was allowing water to seep in, I worried it would ruin the antiques and remaining books. I needed to have a new door installed. I couldn't afford my regular handyman's rates, and Austin, a college freshman, was living in San Luis Obispo, and Zack not yet demonstrated the patience for carpentry. Larry popped into my mind. Even though his carpentry skills and precision were only slightly better than Zack's and mine, I knew he'd be cheap and available, and maybe even willing to barter. Plus, he always had a spare door or toilet hanging around his house.

We hadn't seen each other in a couple of years. He was still doing some handyman jobs for Jane and also trying to make it big in with an alternative energy provider that I suspected was more of a pyramid scheme than a legitimate business. I called, and after the usual pleasantries, I told him my predicament and asked if he'd be willing to barter a cake, or a clothes dryer, or an antique armoire for an hour of handyman work. And did he have a spare door that I could have? I was slowly getting past letting the shame and humiliation of asking others for help stand in my way. A few days later he showed up. After we hugged hello and he said hi to Zack, I followed him out to his truck.

"Do you recognize this door?" he asked. I helped him carry it from his truck to the shed.

"No, but it's pretty."

"It's from your old house on Freeman. There were two of them in your dining room. You had the set removed when you tore down the wall to the kitchen. Remember, I'd asked if I could keep them. I figured I'd use them somewhere down the road."

I pictured the set in my mind. On the frame were a few strips of missing varnish. I remembered how one holiday I'd taped Christmas cards to the glass, and when I ran out of space, to the amber wood. When it came time to remove the cards, the tape pulled off some of the varnish. I now stood by the shed and watched Larry install the door.

"So, what's happening in Larry's world? How's your son?"

He updated me on his son, who still hadn't gone back to school to finish his last semester of college. "Are you dating?" I asked.

"Nah. No time. I don't know if Jane mentioned it, but I got a call from an old girlfriend a while back. She'd been getting beat up by her live-in boyfriend. She and her sixteen-year-old daughter needed a place to live. I finally cleaned up the old cat room for the daughter. Her mom took the other bedroom."

"Wow. That's nice of you. Do you like having roommates?" I thought about how it could have been my sons and me living with Larry. Those days seemed more than a lifetime ago. Standing and watching him unscrew the old door, I felt nothing other than friendship for him now.

"It was fun. Like a readymade family." He handed me the screws as he removed them from the old door hinges. "But the mom went back to the boyfriend."

"What an idiot. And her poor daughter."

"Oh, the daughter is still living with me," he said proudly. He tossed the splintered door into nearby weeds and grabbed the measuring tape.

"What? What do you mean she's still living with you?"

"Her mom and I agreed she was better leaving her daughter with me. I could play dad and keep her out of trouble."

"That's a little strange. Don't you agree?"

"No, not at all," he said. "I'm a good role model. She looks at me like a father figure. Plus, I've got plenty of space in the house, and I make her do chores. I'm pretty stern. If she's out past curfew or doesn't finish her chores, I take away her privileges." I assumed he meant TV or computer time.

Questions I Should Have Asked, #22: Does child protective services allow this kind of unofficial, sketchy living arrangement?

It sounded like a pretty bizarre situation. How could a mom leave her child behind and entrust her underage daughter to the care of a middle-aged man—no matter how far back their friendship went and how good of a role model he prided himself on being? Suddenly, the vibes I was getting from Larry were icky. It was the first time I thought, *I can't believe I ever let him touch me.* There was just something so creepy about him and this sixteen-year-old girl.

He hung the door without a problem, but somehow he messed up the hole he'd drilled for the doorknob. When the wood splintered and the beautiful finish was further ruined, I laughed to myself. *Good ol' Larry. He tries, but he's crap at handyman work.* We visited in the kitchen for a while after he finished installing the door. I was making pancakes for Zack, and Larry turned them down. I was shocked. I couldn't remember him ever refusing anything sweet.

"So, what can I give you?" I asked, sitting down at the table. I was embarrassed as Larry looked around the kitchen. Our living situation had declined from a spacious, custom kitchen on Freeman to this cramped kitchen/dining area that still had a faint smell of death and boasted the original red Formica counters. "Do you need an armoire or an antique vanity? An extra clothes dryer?"

Larry shook his head. "I've already got too much stuff. But if you want to transfer your PG&E account over to my new electrical provider, that would be great." He went into his sales pitch, and I thought, *Shit. What in the hell does Larry know about the utility business?* He claimed I could save a bundle. It was supposed to be a no-brainer: same dependable electricity, but at a reduced rate.

"Are you sure it's legitimate? I don't want any hassles with my electricity."

"It's definitely legitimate. I've already signed up several of the volleyball group."

"Jane?" "Not yet. She's thinking about it."

Why couldn't he simply accept an armoire or the dryer and call us square? Something about Larry's sure bet seemed risky. I was nervous that somehow this new business of his would end up costing me more money. Besides, Larry's knowledge of utilities was probably on par with his knowledge of pool installation and electrical wiring. I pictured myself at a later date, frustrated by one electrical blackout after another, on the phone with some bored PG&E representative and trying to talk my way out of an account reconnection fee.

"Well, let me think about it and do some research. I'll get back to you by next week." I promised to read through the literature he left with me, and we hugged goodbye. I watched him walk to his truck and felt sadness for him and the life he'd carved out for himself.

I never contacted Larry about switching providers. Had he followed up, I would have offered once again one of my antiques or to bake him his favorite German chocolate cake, but I would not abandon PG&E. Months later, I texted Larry to say happy birthday. There was no reply. A couple of months later, I texted to ask if Austin could use him as a job reference. Still no reply. I figured he was pissed that I hadn't kept my end of the bargain. Turned out, that wasn't the case.

chapter eighteen

EVEN BEFORE LARRY and I had split up, we'd stopped spending as much time with Jane. She was focused on recovering from her own financial setbacks and busy launching a business. She was also dating someone new. We rarely spoke or saw each other when she was in the honeymoon phase with a guy. She'd call if she needed help with something, or if this new boyfriend turned out not to be, in fact, Prince Charming but other than that, it could be months before we spoke or saw each other. Plus, I'd quit a book club that she'd invited me to join after having spent months of listening to her talk nonstop about herself during the meetings. It came as a surprise when, after months of silence, she called and invited me to dinner.

Around Jane, I was always self-conscious about how I dressed and looked. She took considerable care in her appearance. She remarked on the appearance of others. I always felt she was secretly judging me by my weight, clothes, parenting, and business success or failure. Surely, she'd notice the weight I'd gained since our last get-together.

"I heard Larry has some teenage girl living with him," I said. Jane finished her first glass of wine and waved the server over to order another.

She shook her head. "Everyone from our volleyball group is pissed off. He promised to have her move out, but I don't think he's done it."

"I'm surprised the mother would allow it. Even as fucked up as she sounds."

Jane nodded and fiddled with her empty wine glass. "He has also pissed off some of our closest friends because at the last volleyball camp out, he kept taking pictures of their young grandkids running around in their swim suits or naked. Everyone started noticing how obsessed he was and made him delete the photos." Before I could pry more details from her, she steered the conversation to her newest boyfriend. "He might be the one," she said. "We've been looking at houses. We're thinking about moving out of the Bay Area." I was both happy for her and envious. She had no difficulty finding boyfriends. But then, the men she dated I never found attractive.

After dinner and before climbing out of my car, she paused. "You really should think about losing weight. I think you'd feel better. Maybe then you'd start dating again."

Jane was always blunt. Even so, her comment stung. I was ashamed but also miffed as I drove away. She never asked how I thought her constant parade of boyfriends might have affected her children, and I never volunteered my thoughts on the matter, though I certainly had my opinions. Obviously, she had been thinking about sharing this advice and figured what better time than right before she hopped out of the car.

Not long after this dinner, I received a text from her asking me to meet her for dinner. I was surprised she'd contacted me again so soon after our last dinner. She said she needed to talk to me about something very important. I had been feeling depressed, and admittedly, also over sharing on Facebook about my funk. I looked at the text and my face was hot with shame. Here would come another unsolicited lecture, this time about how I was humiliating myself on social media and needed to show some pride and discretion.

But curiosity won me over. We met for dinner, and after the usual, "How are the kids? How's work? How's the house?" she said, "I wanted to talk to you tonight because—"

Here it comes, I thought, the lecture about Facebook. Maybe Facebook, my weight, updating my hairstyle, and whatever else she felt needed pointing out. I held my breath.

"Larry has been arrested for possessing child pornography."

"What?" This wasn't about me. I smiled and then frowned. "Our Larry?" I was overcome with both relief and shock. She nodded and reached for her wine. "Holy shit! You're serious?" I knew deep down she was serious. I remembered the creepy vibes I felt the last time I spoke with him. Besides, who joked about something like this? "When?"

"He was part of an FBI raid. They'd been watching him and others for a while."

"Was he . . . did he . . ." I couldn't yet say what was sitting in the pit of my stomach. "Was he just looking at the porn or actually making it?" I finally asked. Why that mattered, I wasn't sure.

"They searched his house," she said, "and found a stockpile of computers containing child pornographic videos."

"A stockpile?" Where did Larry get the money to stockpile a bunch of computers? *What a mother fucking pervert!*

"Do you know how close my sons and I came to moving in with him?" I asked. "Oh my god, we really dodged a bullet."

The server came to take our order, but we asked for a few minutes. While I pretended to look over the entrees, I thought about that first time Larry slept over when my sons were home. Zack had come into my bedroom and laid across the foot of the bed, reading a book for his English class. I was so happy that he liked Larry and felt comfortable around him. It felt as if we were a complete family again. The what-if thoughts made me angry.

"How did you find out about this?" I asked.

"He was doing some work for me. One day, out of the blue, the FBI contacted me."

"Fuck." I imagined opening my front door to find *X-Files* agents Mulder and Scully in their pressed white shirts.

"Larry had told me his computer was broken. He asked to borrow my extra laptop."

I marveled at his audacity to stand in Jane's house and lie to her after everything she'd done for him. She'd found project after project for him so he'd have money to live on. She'd fed him, bought that red truck, invited him to join her and her family on vacations. She introduced him to friends and pawned me off on him.

"Since the laptop was registered to me, the FBI traced it back to me."

"Are you in trouble?" I asked, thinking it might somehow make her an accessory to his crimes.

"No. It's pretty clear I'm not involved."

"So where is he now," I asked.

She took a long drink of her wine and looked around for the server. "In jail in Oakland, awaiting trial."

I tried to imagine Larry just a couple of towns over sitting in a cold cell. Was he being beaten up? Or was he kept in solitary confinement to protect him from the other prisoners? It shocked me that I even cared.

"How is his son handling this?"

She told me she hadn't spoken with him, but assumed it would be a long time, if ever before he faced his family and friends here. After dinner, I drove home imagining horrible scenarios involving Larry and my sons. *I will kill him*, I thought, *if that bastard touched Austin or Zack or took one compromising photo of them*. Zack was watching television when I walked into the house. Austin was still away at college.

"How was dinner with Jane?" he asked.

"Fine." I dropped my purse and keys on the floor. "Guess whose house was raided by the FBI for child pornography."

He muted the television and said, "Larry."

Holy shit! "How did you know it was Larry?"

He shrugged.

"Did he ever touch you?"

"Gross, mom. Of course not."

"You sure."

He nodded.

"Then how did you guess Larry so quickly?"

He shrugged again. I called Austin.

"What are you doing, sweetie?"

"Studying. What are you doing?"

"I just had dinner with Jane. Larry was arrested for child pornography."

Austin laughed.

"It's not funny," I said, trying not to laugh with him. "Did he ever touch you? Or do anything inappropriate?"

"No, mom."

"You would tell me, wouldn't you?"

"Yes."

I felt certain that I would have noticed a shift in my sons' behavior if Larry or anyone else had molested them or done something equally offensive. So I trusted that they were telling the truth.

"Remember that teacher in your elementary school?" I asked Austin. "The one arrested for molesting students? He seemed so nice, so normal. All the kids loved him. I had the biggest crush on him. You just never really know a person."

"How's work?" he asked, changing the subject.

Even though Larry was the sick person for downloading and sharing child pornography, I felt dirty having been associated with him. I felt ashamed that we'd dated, been intimate, and I worried that my kids would feel like we were all less respectable now. I worried that they'd think the only men mom could get were jerks like Mike or perverts like Larry. One more thing to set them apart from their friends. I'd done nothing wrong, though. Okay, I should have asked more questions. There were red flags from the beginning, and yet I chose not to delve further. My indifference could have cost my sons and me greatly. It appeared we were lucky.

chapter nineteen

FOR WEEKS AFTER learning of Larry's arrest and hearing the scant details from Jane, I vacillated between anger and shock. I turned over every memory, starting with our first walk around the Lafayette Reservoir to our more in-depth get-to-know-you conversations. I thought about our trip to Las Vegas for the canceled Cher concert. How Larry had nixed, without hesitation, the cab driver's offer to drop us off at an adult sex club so we could see something different. Larry had been adamant in his refusal. He'd acted so righteous and disgusted. How could I have even suggested we watch a bunch of perverted strangers have sex? I had felt so embarrassed. Now, knowing what I knew about him, I figured he might have been more receptive to a suggestion that we watch some helpless children being raped by adults. *What a sick fucker!*

I stacked every exchange between Larry, Jane, and his volleyball friends in my mind and, like 45s, played one after another, looking for clues. Some creepy underbelly in the music that would have predicted his behavior. Then I looked inwardly at my culpability. Was I simply too trusting or complacent? Should I have cared more, asked harder, deeper questions? Why did you leave Home Depot? Why did you quit coaching? Have you ever spent time in jail or been convicted of a crime? Jane had known Larry for two decades, and yet she'd also been duped. Should I have asked her and his other friends more questions about their shared history? It never occurred to me to ask the kinds of questions that would have been relevant to his situation.

In part, I was lazy. I had never expected much from Larry. I never thought he had much going on outside, and never suspected there was more to him on the inside. A harsh assessment, I supposed. But he seemed like a children's book—large font, lots of white space and simple illustrations. Sure, I'd caught him in a lie about Las Vegas, but that was early on and I didn't really care enough about him or us at the time to be jealous.

In a warped way, I felt guilty. What if my abrupt decision not to move in with Larry and our subsequent breakup made him so lonely and sad that he started watching porn? Okay, that was a ridiculous notion. This wasn't my fault. But what if, out of loneliness and desperation, he got hooked on adult porn, and from there stumbled upon child porn? If my sons and I had been living in the house with him, he might not have been able to pursue this interest. But then again, he had a sixteen-year-old girl living with him, and that didn't deter him.

chapter twenty

IN AUGUST 2013, a few months later, after Jane dropped the Larry bomb at dinner, I was sitting in bed reading the newspaper when I saw the headline: *Child Porn Distributor Gets 15 Years — Man Served Three Years Previously for Statutory Rape.*

Wow, another pervert in Pleasant Hill, I thought. I scanned the article, stopped at Larry's last name, and doubled-back to the Statutory Rape subtitle. *What were they talking about? That couldn't be right. Were there two Lawrence Pallens in Pleasant Hill?* The article claimed Lawrence Pallen had previously spent three years in prison for statutory rape. *What shoddy journalism,* I thought. The reporter had obviously confused his case with another child molester in Pleasant Hill. Surely Larry, Jane, or one of their volleyball friends would have mentioned this prior felony.

The FBI had discovered hidden cameras embedded in his ex-girlfriend's daughter's bathroom wall and underneath their shared bathroom sink. Even though Larry's handyman skills were seriously lacking, especially in terms of electrical work, he somehow figured out how to install a light switch in his bedroom to a camera where he could watch the girl live. *Sick, sick bastard.*

They found videos of his young roommate and photos from a Danville high school volleyball game. Did he attend one of the games and pretend to be a proud parent or uncle filming his daughter from the sidelines? The article said he was part of a peer-to-peer network, sharing online videos of children, including prepubescent minors, engaged in sex acts with adults. Four different computers, seven external storage drives, and four camera memory cards. Four camera memory cards! Was he the sicko behind the camera? Were these pictures he'd taken himself? Were there images of his friend's children and grandchildren from the camp outs?

Reading and rereading the article, I sighed loudly and imagined others feeling as horrified and shocked as I felt. His family and friends must have been calling each other to ask if they'd seen today's paper. His arrest was one of five Bay Area indictments in the U.S. Immigration and Customs Enforcement's Operation Sunflower. One of 246 suspected child porn producers spanning 48 states and six countries. *Operation Sunflower*. How strange. After he'd hung the door on my shed, I painted four huge, bright sunflowers on the glass window. Was there a connection between those flowers and the name of the sting operation?

I leaned back in bed, set aside the paper, and thought, *I've dated and slept with a convicted child pornographer* and *a molester*. My sons and I had almost shared a house, a kitchen, a bathroom with him. How many times had he come to watch my high school divers' practice? No wonder he was such a faithful fan. I tried to recall if he ever photographed any of my divers at practice or a meet, but I couldn't remember an instance where he'd done so. I'd have been mortified if some of their photos or videos were found among the evidence collected.

According to the article, his previous conviction stemmed from inappropriately touching two young girls while working as a volunteer coach and then having sex with a fourteen-year-old volleyball player during a traveling tournament. He later claimed that the rape occurred because of "a little alcohol, a little opportunity, a little braveness." *Darn, I hate when that happens*, I thought, sarcastically—what an asinine comment. *I was just out having a good ol' time with my buds and the next thing I knew, I'd had too much to drink, and I'm molesting a kid. That, my dear Larry,* I thought, *was the lamest excuse I'd ever heard.* Was he really that flippant? *What's the big deal? Just a case of being in the wrong place at the wrong time. You son of a bitch.*

I had always wondered why he had quit drinking. Why didn't I ever ask? Giving up alcohol was a big decision. Usually, there was a matter of hitting bottom, and in my case, I could pinpoint the moment I realized I needed to stop drinking or else I'd never sustain a relationship and have children. What was his bottom? Was it the three years the reporter claimed Larry spent in jail? Or fearing that once released, he might start drinking again, relapse into his old ways, and end up back in jail? Why wasn't he required to register as a sex offender after the first conviction? There was always the unspoken question of why he'd quit coaching girls' volleyball. He'd loved volleyball. He claimed he didn't play anymore because of his bad knees and ankles. I should have probed deeper. It never occurred to me that I needed to be so careful. That he could hide so much and honestly, any curiosity I'd had about Larry's background was fleeting.

If what the journalist reported was accurate, and Larry had spent three years in jail for statutory rape, why would Jane have set me up with him? Surely, she would have known. Surely, she knew there'd be teenagers—boys and girls—at my house while Larry was around. She couldn't have been that cruel, could she? Maybe there was some explanation for all of this. Maybe this alleged rape conviction and prior jail time was indeed careless research. I searched Larry's name on the internet and found only links to this recent article. There were no links relating to this purported earlier arrest and conviction. In my fury, I emailed the reporter to accuse her of sloppy reporting. I insisted she'd confused the two Lawrence Pallens, lumping the rapist in with the child pornographer. She needed to clear up the facts immediately and let me know that the rape charge and conviction were errors. Of course, she never wrote back. She undoubtedly thought I was a hopeless idiot.

I was certain that just like a California wildfire on a windy day, news had spread and leaped across roads and cities. The volleyball group must have been calling, texting, and emailing each other since the first person opened their newspaper and read the headline. *WTF? Larry did what? Are we talking about the same Larry? He seemed like such a nice guy. But there was that time . . . Holy crap, I just heard and was about to call you!* As I thought about all of his friends contacting one another, trading information and speculation as one did when something this juicy disrupted a close community, I realized that I hadn't heard from Jane all day. The silence was astounding.

In the decade when Jane's and my friendship was the strongest, starting with our kids' preschool days, how many times had she called or stopped by my house to divulge private things about herself, her love life, her finances, her family, her children, our mutual friends? No detail had ever seemed too intimate. No boundaries were too sacred. I had admitted to her that Larry had cum only once and that our romantic life was fairly dull. That he'd go on forever and ever, and never climax. That he'd switch from one position to the next, and while enduring endless acrobatics in bed, I'd pray, *Oh, Christ Almighty, get it over with already!* She never said directly, "Perhaps he's not attracted to you. Maybe you don't turn him on." But that was the vibe I got from her.

Jane had advised me on my career, my parenting, my love life, my clothes, my weight, my finances, etc., whether or not I'd asked for her input. So why now the reticence? Wouldn't a friend be concerned about how I was handling the news?

Furious and baffled, I grabbed my phone.

"Hey, it's Marie. Did you see the article?"

"About Larry?"

No, about the moon landing, I thought angrily. "Yes. Is it true that he raped a fourteen-year-old volleyball player and spent three years in jail?"

"Apparently."

"You didn't know that he'd been in jail?"

"Well . . . I knew about him going to jail. But I thought it was only for about six months and for embezzling from Home Depot."

I laughed at the absurdity of her casual reply. "And *embezzling* wasn't something you felt you needed to disclose when you set us up?"

"I figured he told you about it."

"But shouldn't you have verified? Maybe you should have asked, *So I guess Larry told you about his jail time?* That's a pretty big detail to leave out."

"I just thought you knew."

I shook my head. *That's it. I just thought you knew. Fuck you!*

"You knew he lied to me about going to Las Vegas with friends when he'd really gone with his ex-girlfriend. And he lied to you when you asked if he'd told me since we'd just started dating seriously. There was a clear history of lying."

"I didn't feel like it was my business."

Bullshit. If the tables were turned, she'd be furious that I had withheld information on whom exactly she was getting involved with.

"It's true then? The reporter wasn't confusing Larry with some other Larry? He really did all those things they printed in the newspaper? He really spent three years in jail."

"It appears so."

Why hadn't any of his friends ever pulled me aside at a party or at the river camp out to ask if I knew about Larry's history? Or let something slip after a few drinks? That weird guy at the camp out who told us about masturbating to stay awake on long drives. Surely his boundaries were a bit blurred and he'd be the most likely to let this bit of history slip out in some warped get-to-know-you conversation.

"Did all his volleyball friends and family know?"

"No. It looks like only Rodney and Julie knew the truth. The others like me, apparently, believed the Home Depot story."

"Have you seen him since his arrest?"

She told me he asked her, via his attorney, to write a letter on his behalf. His attorney claimed that if some of his long-time friends would vouch for Larry, it might help lessen his sentencing. Surprisingly, Jane had refused to write anything that might appear to condone his sick behavior. Apparently, she had some scruples.

The deception and betrayal felt personal, not only by Jane but by the friends I'd made through Larry. One thing was clear to me as we ended the call: you can tell a lot about what a person thinks of you by whom they set you up with. Obviously, Jane didn't think very highly of me. It was time to cut toxic people out of my life.

chapter twenty-one

WHEN I FIRST READ the *Contra Costa Times* article about Larry's conviction and his fifteen-year jail sentence, I felt like one of those shocked neighbors or exes captured on television after an arrest.

"He seemed like such a harmless guy," I might have said on camera, squinting into the morning sun. "He was always so nice to my sons . . ." Or I maybe I would have scratched my head and mused, "I remember this dumb comment he made about my tennis shoes. I'd just been hired to coach the district's high school dive teams and he thought my scuffed shoes made me look unprofessional. Funny, given what we now know about his past, this statutory rape business." In Larry's warped mind, did he consider wearing clean white shoes more important than keeping his dick out of the young girls whom the parents and schools had entrusted him to coach? I admittedly found, at a distance, some irony in his comment. However, when I thought of all the times he'd attended my dive practices and watched these young, barely clad children and teenagers, his green eyes on their youthful bodies, I felt angry. Did the sick bastard get aroused? Did he use these images later when he whacked off? I felt culpable for giving him an excuse, an opportunity to be within eyesight of these children as if I brought the fox to the henhouse. I felt so fortunate, for myself, these kids, and their families, that he was never alone with them.

Thinking back on our thirteen-month relationship, and considering his convictions, things had made sense. If he got off sexually by looking at young children engaging in sexual activity, and if he got off by molesting teenage girls, wouldn't it be reasonable that he'd have difficulty climaxing with an adult? There wasn't anything taboo about having sex with a consenting adult. Not like the thrill of being part of a covert club or the excitement of not knowing what the next click would bring.

After getting what little information Jane had to share, I contacted the wife of Larry's best friend, Rodney. She said that Larry had confided in Rodney and her about the statutory rape conviction years back when he was first arrested. They had been "very disappointed" at the time. He'd claimed it was a terrible mistake—molesting three underage girls and having sexual relations with one fourteen-year-old—and they had believed him. *What the fuck!*

"We both assumed you knew about his history," she said, adding that it wasn't until this second conviction that they understood the severity of his problem. But they were still sticking by him and had even visited him twice in the Oakland jail. I'd later learned that they even offered to allow Larry to live at their house with an ankle tracking bracelet while he served his prison sentence. Was this level of support admirable? At what point, I wondered, did their unwavering support veer toward aiding and abetting?

I was astounded by the fact he'd spent three years in jail before we'd met and not once in our thirteen months had he alluded to his incarceration, nor to his arrest and the subsequent scandal among the affected families, or to any of the experiences that surely must have regularly orbited his mind. Was living in jail the reason he'd adopted such low standards of living? Spam. A stinky cat piss house. Free county medical care, mooching off friends and family. Assuming he was already trafficking in child porn when we were dating, I have imagined he knew, on some level, there was a chance he'd get caught and end up back in jail. No need to make more than the absolute minimum to support himself. He most likely figured he didn't need to worry or save for retirement.

I have wondered about his adult son. Surely this ordeal has adversely affected him. Did he receive hate mail and personal threats like those received by other families of accused sexual predators that I'd read about? Was there any contact now between the two? If Larry were my father, would I be able to wash my hands clean of him? Pretend he didn't exist? Or could I find some compassion, some reason to remain in contact? Not long after Larry's conviction, I located his son via Facebook and sent him a private message. Something like: "I hope you are doing well. I know this must be a difficult time for you. You have a lot of family and friends in the Bay Area who care a great deal about you. I hope you'll find comfort in knowing that and keep in touch with them." He never replied. I didn't really expect he would.

Was it all worth it? I wished I could ask Larry. *Worth the loss of your freedom and presumably your relationships with your family and friends?*

chapter twenty-two

THE CHRISTMAS SEASON after Larry's sentencing, I was selling my handmade wire baskets and jewelry at a neighborhood holiday craft fair when a mom I knew from my sons' preschool spotted me from across the room and came over. We hugged hello, and after we caught up on our kids, jobs, lives in general, Sue asked, "Are you dating anyone?" The last boyfriend she'd met was Mike.

"Not at the moment." I wondered if a few years could be accurately defined as a moment. "I was dating this guy that Jane set me up with. Remember Jane? Your favorite person?"

Sue rolled her eyes. Jane's son Josh had teased Sue's son about his narrow eyelids so relentlessly that he'd subjected himself to two surgeries to enlarge the openings and hopefully stop Josh's teasing.

"Anyway, I know you don't like Josh, and for good reason. But this guy Jane set me up with has been arrested and sentenced to fifteen years in prison for child pornography."

"Holy shit. Are you serious?" she asked, trying not to laugh. It really wasn't funny, but we had a shared history of hearing the most unexpected things come out of each other's mouths and bursting into laughter.

"Ironically, I broke up with him because he ate Spam."

"Spam. Seriously?" I wasn't sure if it was that she was surprised he ate Spam, or if she was shocked I'd been so shallow to dump a man just because he liked canned meat. She set her purse down next to my display. She was staying put for the story of Larry and Marie. When I got to the punchline, for that is what Larry had become, I added, "Here I thought he was a loser for having no taste, and yet he's a total pervert with a previous incarceration."

We laughed and then Sue asked, "Remember that preschool teacher? The one you had such a crush on."

"Of course," I said. "All the kids, including my sons, loved him. He was so adorable in his white painter's pants and sneakers. He acted like a big kid: rowdy, loud, silly, and always bubbly. I used to watch him play dodgeball on the playground before school and think, he'd be a fun boyfriend if he weren't married." Hearing these words said aloud, I wondered if there was some reason I was drawn to these creeps or was the world just full of creeps.

"I'd say you lucked out there," she said. This beloved teacher's arrest had shocked and divided the private, close-knit school—one faction set against the other. For a while, there were rumors of potential bankruptcy from a lawsuit that was eventually settled.

"I must have a knack for finding the pervert in the group." To prove my point, I shared the story of my sons' math teacher who, like the preschool teacher, was extremely playful and popular with the children. Worrying that Zack might have a difficult transition to middle school, as did Austin, I applied for and got a substituting job at the district.

"This teacher was so handsome," I told my friend. "I had a crush on him. Not only did the kids love him, but the staff adored him as well. I'd sit in the lunch room and watch the popular group of teachers chat and play shuffle board. He was always the center of attention."

I told her about the sofa in the back of the classroom and how I thought it odd.

"True," she agreed and smiled because she suspected what was coming. Sue and I did not lack empathy as much as we both had our own failures, and realized some comfort in knowing our failures paled compared to others'.

"Turns out this math teacher had had sex with a fourteen-year-old student he was tutoring. Investigators found semen on the sofa. The sicko had sent the victim hundreds of sexually explicit texts."

"I think I read about him."

"Probably. Sadly, there are so many in the news these days. It's hard to keep track of them. But off to jail went another one of my crushes."

"You should hire yourself out as a pedophile crime-stopper," Sue said. We both giggled and looked around to make sure we weren't being overheard. It wasn't the venue to be having such a bizarre conversation. "They could place you in a room with a bunch of middle-aged men and simply arrest the ones you find attractive."

It was entertaining, for a few minutes, to make light of what was truly an awful situation. But then the reality of these terrible acts collided with our merriment and the laughing stopped. There was no denying it was a sick and terrible fact that children aren't able to attend school or enjoy sports or participate in group activities free of worry that some pervert might be lurking nearby.

After Sue left my table to browse the other displays, I thought about the math teacher and wondered what happened to the wife and daughters he left behind. Do these men, and sometimes women, ever think about the emotional and financial hit to their loved ones' lives? Do they ever consider the crushing sadness and anger these people face when they wake up and learn that everything they *knew* to be true is false? To find themselves often abandoned by their community and friends in an assumption of complicity? That the husband or father they loved and considered a decent human being was really a monster. The colleague they admired and trusted was a very flawed and deceitful man. The humiliation. The betrayal. The anger. The fear. This was the wake Larry and his kind leave behind.

I've often wondered if Larry ever had any empathy for his victims. Did he ever look into these children's eyes and shudder in horror? Was he ever able to see the damage he and others like him had done to the children's self-esteem? Did he understand, even now, as he sits in jail, that he stole any hope that these children would ever feel truly safe again? Could he, in his mind's eye, see the barrier he'd created between these children and all others? Was there ever any consideration of the damage to his own family and friends? Or did he simply think to himself, "I wish I hadn't been caught," and still have no regrets?

chapter twenty-three

THE WHOLE LARRY-SITUATION set in motion a huge upset to my self-esteem. How could I have been so fooled? Some days it felt so surreal, as unlikely and bizarre as learning one of my favorite childhood TV characters, sweet and simple Gomer Pyle, was actually running a child pornography outfit behind his filling station, unbeknownst to his friends and family in Mayberry. Larry's niceness and harmlessness were simply a mirage. The sick bastard probably never really cared about my sons or me. And his biggest legacy as a boyfriend? I lost all confidence that I would ever again really know and trust someone enough to let them close to me. Was I even capable of protecting myself from harm? If nothing else, the whole sorted mess left me angry at myself for demonstrating, repeatedly, such bad judgment in men, for not thinking I was worth more than a guy dumped in my lap by a *friend* who really never had my best interest at heart. A guy that someone with more self-worth would never have allowed past the "It's nice to meet you" stage.

Once or twice a year, in a fit of loneliness, I've perused the profiles in Match.com and other singles website. But after an hour or so of scanning and reading profiles, resetting age and geographic parameters to expand my results, I'd give up. Who really knew what lurked behind that endless checkerboard of faces and fun *facts*? How much more careful did I need to be? What did I need to do differently next time? Sure, I could tell myself to pay closer attention to those nagging feelings I sometimes got when things didn't seem quite right. Remind myself to be more vigilant. Ask more questions. Trust my instincts. But how would I know what to be curious about? (Why does this guy have a pink nightgown hanging in his closet?) Must I investigate every brief pause that flashed across my mind? (He can only climax when he fears getting caught?) Some things seemed so far out of the realm of possibilities that I wouldn't naturally think to delve into it. It never occurred to me to ask: *So Larry, have you checked out any good child pornography today?*

Years ago, right before Mike, I dated the divorced father of a child I'd known for a couple of years through one of the organizations I was involved in. The guy seemed like a good father. He regularly attended events and socialized with the other parents. He was ambitious, smart, and athletic. We went on a few dates and then slept together. That first time, he held my arms against the mattress and manically pumped while yelling, "Cum . . . Cum . . . Cum!" It was a bizarre and frightening experience. While he pumped and barked at me, I looked into the man's angry Doberman Pincher face and thought, if I wasn't feeling relaxed enough to cum before he started yelling, I surely wasn't going to cum now. I realized later, after reflecting on his behavior in my bed, that I'd detected something aggressive and insistent about this guy from the moment he rushed over to introduce himself at an event. I'd written it off as confidence and interest and told myself not to worry. After all, he was a dad in my community. This man wasn't my dream guy, but he'd made me laugh. We were both starting a business and struggling with similar start-up issues, so we commiserated and offered each other advice. For months, I talked myself away from the exit, thinking perhaps I was being rash. Maybe he had a slightly kinky side, but nothing more than that. Surely, he wouldn't hurt me. I knew his ex-wife, his kids. He wouldn't risk his reputation. Would he?

Partly, I would admit now, I was curious. I have always been curious why people, myself included, behave the way we do. Why do we make the choices we make? How do we justify our actions? How can we look at a blue sky and insist it is green? Or how can we press one foot to another's throat and yet deny ever having caused any harm? I'm curious why we go to great lengths to hide who we really are. Obviously, to avoid being shunned, but still, is it worth the trouble? I'm intrigued by people who look so cookie-cutter and harmless, like this guy, but then you scratch below the surface and find things that surprise, even shock you. It takes such energy to deceive people. It amazes me that we, as an evolved, over-scheduled race, really have that much energy and free time to hide our true selves.

I had a few more dates with this guy. The next time he pulled my hair during sex and I jerked my head out of his grip. He slapped my butt, and I said, "No." My curiosity was replaced with fear. It felt like I was under the attack of one of the firefighter's hoses that unpredictably flies through the air, coming at you from all directions. This final time, he terrified me, and I pulled away, put a safe distance between us, and asked, "Is this a *thing* for you? Do you get off on hurting women? Because I'm not into that at all. And I can't relax because I don't trust you."

How would I have ever known by looking at this man that he got off on hurting women? I have never been naïve enough to think that S & M was something that existed only in novels and movies. I just hadn't encountered it before. It wasn't something men put on their Match.com profile. At least I hadn't seen it mentioned. It was not as if they said, "Hey, my name is Joe Blow, and I'd like to spank you and pull your hair." Or "My name is Larry and I like to watch young children having sexual relations with adults."

When I think about dating, my fears rear up and take a big bite out of my self-esteem. *Am I like a house that has sat on the market for too long?* I wonder. Buyers have come and gone, contracts have been entered into and reneged. A house that languishes because buyers see the stats: 60, 80, 120 days on the market, and assume there's some major structural damage, or it's a money pit, or someone died inside, or there's something unsavory about the neighborhood. Surely if this house were desirable, a good find, someone would have snatched it up. I've fallen out of contract so often I fear I'm doomed to languish forever. At times of optimism, I think I could rework the foundation, throw on a paint job, update the garden, basically just spruce up and give myself more curb appeal, but then again, what if I do all that, and the only suitors I attract are wolves?

A friend I'd known a few years once asked me to go to Planned Parenthood and take an STD test, giving them her name so she could show the results to a man she'd met online and had just started dating. Apparently, Planned Parenthood doesn't require a photo ID. Even though she'd been quite promiscuous, she was sure she didn't have AIDS but wasn't positive that the herpes result wouldn't come back, she explained, as a false-positive since she'd had shingles. This was a woman whom I admired. I was completely aghast that she'd ask a friend to be an accomplice in such a dirty, deceptive trick. Perhaps my often-warped sense of humor had led her to believe that my morals were very flexible. "I'm sorry," I told her, "but I can't do that. That's so dishonest and unfair to the guy. Besides, do you really want to start a relationship with a lie? What if you have herpes and he contracts it? What if he found out I'd helped you out like this? We'd both look like horrible people. Plus, there must be some sort of law against that."

Thinking back on my friend's bizarre request, I figured the man, her potential lover, never thought to say, "Just to be clear, please make sure it's your test results and not that of one of your friends."

The million-dollar question in my mind now: how can I ever be certain that I really know someone well enough to let them into my life? How can I know that a person is truly the person being advertised? That they are not simply a mirage or a lousy trick?

chapter twenty-four

I STILL THINK OF LARRY often when in a reflective mood. Not fondly, obviously. More as a curiosity or befuddlement. Or I might sit on the BART platform, waiting for the next train to San Francisco, and suddenly a scented breeze will sweep past my nose. Some man might be wearing his cologne, or something similar. It always irked me when Larry called it "putting on my stink." It made him sound like such a hick.

Other times I might talk to a coworker who says she's never eaten dinner in a restaurant alone, adding that the thought of it freaks her out. I'll remember how after Larry and I broke up, I had to get used to going out to dinner and movies alone again when my kids were with their dad. How I didn't miss Larry, per se, I just missed having another companionable adult by my side. And of course, every time I read about a coach, teacher, priest, parent, or some other adult who'd been caught molesting a child or caught with a computer full of child pornography, Larry leaped to mind. And I'd wonder, once again: *How could I have been so oblivious?*

Sometimes, for no reason I can identify, I'll look at my watch and think to myself, I wonder what Larry is doing right now. Is he in his cell waiting for dinner? Has he been assigned some sort of prison job, maybe washing dishes or scrubbing toilets? There would be some justice in making him chisel dried shit off of steel toilet bowls and mop up piss by a bunch of serial rapists and murderers. He has probably made friends by now and is no doubt boring the crap out of them with the minutiae of his day spent cleaning toilets. In my more disturbing musing, I'll wonder if he's someone's boy toy. If he gets passed around does he worry about getting HIV? Does he fight the men off, or has he learned just to acquiesce and get it over with? I figure if he's lucky, once the others have had their fun or pleasure, they've moved on to the next new prisoner? No one, even Larry, deserved to be raped. He was a human being, after all, no matter how tragic his story.

I met a former warden of a Northern California prison at a retreat. I told her about Larry and his conviction and asked if she thought he was getting raped. She said, "Without a doubt. Sexual offenders who target children are at the bottom of the pecking order, the top of the most hated and abused." This hatred and intolerance seemed justified. However, it seemed hypocritical that a man jailed for, say, murdering another adult might think he's somehow better than a child molester or pornographer. The act of raping or harming a child is deplorable, especially since they can't protect themselves, but isn't it also harmful to a child to murder their parent and deny them the right to a mom or dad? The thin thread of compassion I occasionally felt for Larry and what he must face in his daily incarceration disappeared after reading the accounts of child pornography victims who spend their childhoods and adult lives worrying about being recognized from one of the videos floating around the internet. It rips my heart to shreds to hear the still terrified victims acknowledge that the existence of these images documenting and showcasing their abuse and the fact that they are shared like trading cards is worse than the actual abuse.

I often wonder if Larry will die before his release from prison. He'll be seventy-five then. I think that if I were him, I'd hope to die in prison. It's difficult to imagine coming out at retirement age and starting over with nothing but a pittance of social security from his Home Depot days. Of course, that would be the least of his worries.

Why do I now even waste another minute thinking about this guy? The simple answer is that I'm looking for closure. I want to lay all the evidence on the table, examine each piece, and try to figure out how I missed so many signs. I want to know if my radar is completely whacked. How did he pull off so many lies? Dupe so many people—not just me? I have been deceived by men before, the usual offenders: married men who pose as single, men with strange sexual proclivities, single men who only seem sincere, but never have I been deceived to this degree. Being blindsided has left me frozen with doubt and fear when it comes to men. Why isn't there a litmus test to weed out the child pornographers, rapists, and other creeps?

And finally, I wonder if Larry ever truly cared about my sons and me—or were we simply part of his ruse? Was he only in it for the free meals and vacations, the cakes and pie, the easy companionship?

In 2016, I was driving for Uber while between jobs. One of my greatest fears, besides being murdered or raped on the job, was picking up someone I knew from a time when I lived a completely different lifestyle. One Saturday evening, I pulled up to an apartment building and my breath caught with mortification when I recognized a face among the four young adults standing at the curb. Jane's son, Josh. Here I was, his former classmate's mom and former neighbor, driving a taxi. While Jane and Josh's stepdad had retired comfortably to their rancher in Northern California, I was living in a shitty part of Pleasant Hill and eating energy bars from Chevron to tide me over during my eight-hour shifts. Had Jane told him I'd recently emailed her to borrow money? I'd exhausted every reasonable option I could think of, sold almost everything of value I owned, and finally, in a panic, I pitched aside my pride and emailed Jane. Had she told her son how she'd declined my request and wished me luck with my job search?

When Josh recognized me, he told the other guys to sit in the back and he sat in the front. We hugged hello. Though embarrassed by the Uber logo on my windshield, I was genuinely happy to see Josh. He told me he'd finished college and was working in San Francisco. He seemed so happy. I told his friends how I'd always been so fond of Josh, that he was such a smart, curious kid. I teased him about some of the antics from his childhood. As we approached their destination, a comedy club in Pleasanton, I said, "So do you ever hear anything about Larry?"

"No. That whole situation was weird."

"It was definitely a shocker. Who knew Larry had it in him to be such a perv?"

Josh laughed. "I remember when I was in high school and my mom caught me downloading porn. She was furious." Josh's friends snickered in the backseat. Josh shrugged them off and continued, "Larry was working on one of his projects around our house and my mom told him what I'd been doing. So weirdly enough, when she wasn't around, he offered to show me how to clear my browsing history so she couldn't see the sites I'd visited. I remembered being so surprised, one, that he was so adept at working a computer, and two, that here was an adult condoning the act of watching porn and teaching me how not to get caught."

I shook my head and laughed along with Josh.

"What a numbnuts," I said. "Great role model."

That evening, after I met my daily Uber goal of one hundred dollars, I went home and sat at my computer to enjoy a couple of hours of mindless social media and internet surfing. My cats laid at my feet as I surfed halfheartedly from Facebook to Instagram to CNN news. I kept thinking about how Larry had taught Josh to clear his browsing history. Jane had done so much for that sick bastard, and there he was undermining her, helping her son to defy her, and encouraging him in unhealthy behavior.

How was it that so few people knew about his first conviction? Didn't Megan's Law require that convicted child molesters register on the State of California Sex Offenders website? I typed *Lawrence Pallen* into meganlaw.ca.gov and got the message: No offenders matched your search. I typed *Larry Pallen*. Nothing. I typed the name of another known local convicted sex offender and got six hits. It made no sense. How did Larry skirt that requirement after his first conviction? Was he convicted before the law took effect? I opened another browser and typed Lawrence Pallen. By page ten of the results, I had found nothing relating to my Larry. I added "arrest" after his name and there he was at the top of the results: *Pleasant Hill man sentenced to 15 years in prison for distributing child* …. and then, holy shit, another article.

East Bay Volleyball Coach Jailed / Alameda man is charged with molesting 2 girls

Henry K. Lee, Chronicle Staff Writer

Published 4:00 am PST, Thursday, December 23, 1999

1999-12-23 04:00:00 PDT ALAMEDA — An East Bay coach accused of molesting a teenage girl on his volleyball team was jailed yesterday after being charged with having sex with her during a trip and molesting another girl at his home.

Top of Form

Bottom of Form

Larry Edmund Pallen, 46, of Alameda was ordered held in lieu of $105,000 bail by Alameda County Superior Court Judge Jeffrey Allen after a prosecutor outlined new charges against the former coach for the Oakland-based Club Kalani, saying that the case so far may be only "the tip of the iceberg."

"He essentially ruined two girls' lives, and we want to prevent that from happening in the future," Assistant District Attorney John Jay told the judge before Pallen was taken into custody. "He presents a risk to the community."

After Pallen was under investigation for allegedly molesting a 16-year-old girl at his home, he sent several pages to a 14-year-old with whom he allegedly had sex with during a team trip to Davis "to dissuade her from cooperating with police," Jay said.

Pallen's attorneys, Dirck Newburg of Berkeley and Sal Balistreri of San Francisco, argued unsuccessfully that their client, a divorced father of a 16-year-old boy, should remain free.

They said Pallen had strong community ties to Alameda, had no criminal history, and had voluntarily resigned after four years of coaching with the club which travels throughout the state to compete.

"This is the first time he's been accused of anything," Balistreri said. "He's (dissociated) himself from the volleyball club. He will not contact anyone."

In court last week, Pallen was charged with one felony count each of lewd and lascivious conduct and penetration with a foreign object for alleged acts with the 14-year-old girl.

Yesterday, Pallen was charged in an amended nine-count criminal complaint for alleged acts involving the girl and a 16-year-old girl who had been under his supervision.

Pallen was accused of rubbing the 14-year-old's breasts and digitally penetrating her while the two were alone in his Alameda home in January.

He was also charged with having sex with the younger girl twice during a team sleepover in a condominium during a tournament at the University of California at Davis in June and July. While two female chaperones slept in an adjacent bedroom, Pallen allegedly had sex with the girl in a separate bedroom, fondled her breasts, and digitally penetrated her, Jay said.

The girl recorded each act in Alameda and Davis in her diary, the prosecutor said.

The complaint yesterday described, for the first time, allegations of molestation involving a 16-year-old girl. Pallen was charged with two counts of oral copulation for alleged acts at his home in July 1998. He was also accused of misdemeanor child molestation for rubbing the girl's breasts and putting his hand in her pants between June and October.

Alameda police are interviewing the three dozen other girls that Pallen has coached during his tenure.

Current team members spoke with counselors on Sunday, and their parents were to meet with club director Roy Ching last night. Many of the girls and their parents feel "betrayed and shocked," Ching said. "It's devastating to me, too, because I've known this person for so long."

I read the article once, my heart pounding more and more after each disgusting detail. I thought about Larry sleeping in his cold cell. How could he have done such things? None of the acts mentioned in the article were one-offs. He'd had time between one event and the next to think about what he was doing and stop himself. My fury soon turned to Jane. She had to have known he wasn't arrested and sentenced for embezzlement. Surely every fucking person on their volleyball team—including the man that coached with Larry and played with Jane's group and who was even now still standing by his man—had read this article, shared their suspicions, observations, and facts over the coming days, weeks, or months. My hands trembled as I reread the article. Did Jane secretly hate me? Want to humiliate and hurt me? Surely there was some ill will brewing, because otherwise, how could she have set me up with this loser? This cruel, sick fuck? Molesting girls who were his own son's peers. Kids he'd been entrusted to protect.

As I sat at my computer fuming, I thought about calling and cussing her out. I wanted her to explain to her husband why her friend Marie was calling at midnight and yelling on the phone like a madwoman. But I figured I'd just look like more of a fool than I already did. I composed a hateful email in my mind, but my hands were shaking so badly it would have been nearly impossible to type. I thought about printing out the article and sending it to her with something hurtful written at the top. But I realized, she wouldn't care. She obviously had some faulty wiring in her brain that allowed her to believe what she wanted to believe, even if it was telling herself, "Well, Marie should have done more due diligence. I'm not her mother. She's a grown woman who can look out for herself."

My mind slowly numbed from the swirling anger and hurt. I breathed deeply a few times and picked up Toby, who was rubbing his body against my leg.

"Come see, sweetie." I cuddled him in my lap and kissed his fur like a crazy cat lady. His sister meowed and nudged my foot. She hated to be left out. I rubbed her orange back with my socked foot and told her to wait her turn. Proving the theory, once again, that cuddling with an animal had an incredibly calming effect. As the cats and I climbed into bed, I realized that the best thing for me was just to say goodbye forever to my friendship with Jane and learn from the entire Larry/Jane experience. Some people are incapable of changing. To talk to Jane and salvage a friendship that she clearly didn't value would have been like throwing a life jacket to a ship that had already sunk to the bottom of the ocean and taken all with it.

chapter twenty-five

GROWING UP, I HAD so many secrets. Each secret carried with it shame and fear. Shame and fear about feelings I'd had or deeds I'd done and shame and fear for things others had done to me, themselves, or others.

At Catechism, when my class prepared for the Sacrament of Confirmation, I became overwhelmed with fear. I begged my parents to let me quit attending Catechism. I promised to homeschool myself with the books I'd found on our shelves from my parent's Catholic studies of their youth. And when begging didn't work, I simply refused to attend another class. I knew that making your Confirmation meant going to confession. I was petrified of the idea of having to admit my secret thoughts and bad deeds to a priest, a man whom, I believed, had been given the power by God to decide the fate of my soul. Even though I now understand that the bad deeds of your average eight or nine-year-old aren't usually on the scale of actions that will get one thrown out of church or banned from heaven, I still felt in my heart as a young girl that I was a bad person. If I wasn't a bad person, then what could have explained the constant abuse I suffered? Surely, I had done something to deserve every strike—physical or verbal—against me.

After publishing two memoirs, I learned, that there are repercussions to telling the truth and opening the Kimono. Some friends, family, colleagues, and strangers have judged me. Some friendships were lost or permanently damaged. My sons, friends, and family have, unfortunately, suffered collateral damage. But I also saw some friendships strengthened. Respect, in some circles, earned. The liberation from self-loathing and fear was greater than I'd ever anticipated. I have made myself vulnerable and availed my flaws to scrutiny. Tested friends and family, perhaps, to find the limits of their love, respect, and acceptance. I've noticed, repeatedly, how my honesty often breeds trust, and likewise, openness and vulnerability in people. People have told me amazing things, entrusted me with secrets they'd never shared with anyone else. I have kept their secrets safe.

Larry, however, never trusted me with his secrets. I supposed for him to do so would have required a willingness or desire to change and accept the repercussions of outing himself.

One of the biggest secrets I kept as a young child was once when I was in first grade, my best friend and I used to cut across an open field of a neighborhood farm on our walk home. One day a teenager, judging by his height, stopped in our path. My friend and I froze, the weeds reaching to our knees. The boy stared at me, his face completely blank, and then, before I could dodge him, he kicked me in my crotch. As the sheer force of his boot knocked me to the ground, my friend ran. She didn't stop running, I suspect until she reached her house. The boy never said a word. He walked around me, leaving me gasping in the trampled weeds. The pain was excruciating. I hugged myself as I trembled and cried, wondering what I'd done to this boy to deserve to be hurt like this. I didn't even know him. He didn't know me. Sometimes life feels like that—getting kicked in the crotch by a stranger.

I can remember wiping away my tears and walking home as my chin wobbled in my attempt to hold myself together. I walked into the kitchen, kissed my mother hello as if nothing bad had just happened and went upstairs to my bedroom. There was blood in my underwear. I touched between my legs and found I was bruised and swollen. I can't recall what thoughts and fears ran through my mind that made me disinclined to tell my parents about the boy kicking me in my private area. I suspected my friend didn't tell her parents either, because there was no concerned call made to our house that evening, or ever. My friend and I never spoke of that afternoon, and in a way, we had made a pact in our silence. We walked home separately thereafter. No more short cuts. No more cutting through the woods. We took the sidewalks now.

I'm sure it was shame and fear that kept me quiet. Fear that I'd done something wrong, maybe something as simple as just being me, a person who could instill such hatred and disgust in a boy. From time to time, I've thought about him, by now a man, and wonder, is he a father? Is he successful? A pillar of his community? Or is he living under a bridge or rotting in jail? You just never know. Maybe he was sharing a cell with Larry. Stranger things have happened.

People are so often, it has seemed, transparent around me, that I don't always bother to look beyond what they show unless I can't help but spot cracks in their veneer. I know some people are sneaky. Some delude themselves and others. Some are indeed bad people. Yet wouldn't it be nice to take people at face value? Expect and receive honesty from others? Being vigilant and suspicious all the time is a lot of work. It takes the fun out of living in the moment. Yet I know to hope for full transparency and honesty is naïve.

I recently searched the internet for "How well can you ever know someone?" and found over 270 million results—an unimaginable wealth of thought and content generated around this universal question.

There are probably thousands of quizzes online, in books and magazines that one can find on people starting a new relationship. Most of the ones I've sampled wouldn't have really helped me to get a true sense of Larry. SignUpGenius.com posts one hundred questions to help readers get to know someone:

Who is your hero?

If you could live anywhere, where would it be?

What is your biggest fear?

What is your favorite family vacation?

What would you change about yourself if you could?

What really makes you angry?

What motivates you to work hard?

What is your favorite thing about your career?

What is your biggest complaint about your job?

What is your proudest accomplishment?

What is your child's proudest accomplishment?

What is your favorite book to read?

What makes you laugh the most?

What was the last movie you went to? What did you think?

What did you want to be when you were small?

What does your child want to be when he/she grows up?

If you could choose to do anything for a day, what would it be?

What is your favorite game or sport to watch and play?

Would you rather ride a bike, ride a horse, or drive a car?

What would you sing at Karaoke night?

What two radio stations do you listen to in the car the most?

Which would you rather do: wash dishes, mow the lawn, clean the bathroom, or vacuum the house?

If you could hire someone to help you, would it be with cleaning, cooking, or yard work?

If you could only eat one meal for the rest of your life, what would it be?

Who is your favorite author?

Most of the questions wouldn't reveal much. Some are actually stupid. But look at question number 25. Say in an attempt to know the real Larry—from his greatest dreams to his most private fears, every

149

common and uncommon fact about him, his history, his interests, his tastes, and so on—I had asked him this question: Who is your favorite author? And instead of saying James Patterson, he had said, "Vladimir Nabokov." Perhaps even added: "He gets me. His protagonist in *Lolita*, Humbert Humbert, and I are kindred spirits. We both desire to know, in the most biblical sense, the ripening beauty of a nymphet."

Well, that answer would have been pretty revealing. But who would give such an honest answer? Some questions in the list and other similar lists, if answered honestly, could have given me some greater insight into Larry and his past. But not enough to really understand him and what made him tick. Perhaps from this list, I should have honed in on these questions: What is your biggest fear? What would you change about yourself if you could? What really makes you angry? And some of my own: If you were given one do-over, one mulligan, what would it be? Have you ever hurt anyone and wished you could undo it? In what way did you hurt them? What are you most ashamed of? Have you ever been in prison? Have you ever been charged and/or found guilty of a crime? Would a school district hire you to coach after running a background check? What would you do if you found out someone had molested or hurt your child or someone you loved? Do you look at pornography?

And if this man didn't take offense, didn't walk away, or run out of shame and fear, if he had actually answered my questions, I should have paid close attention to his face and body language to make sure they supported his words.

I've done a thorough autopsy of Larry and my relationship, and the part Jane played in there being a Larry and Marie. Driven by great curiosity, anger, and fear, I've poked, prodded, lifted, dissected, and examined evidence, conversations, and memories under a microscope. The answers I've found have only led to more questions. So, if I could sit across from Larry in his cell right now, I might ask: "Please tell me what I could have asked you, point-blank, that would have unlocked an impeachable fact about your true nature? What were the questions you most feared I'd ask you? When we had stood outside of Starbucks and I disclosed my bipolar diagnosis, did you consider, even briefly, telling me about your past? Did you consider the victims and the hurt you were causing? Have you even an ounce of regret in what you've done to the children in those photos and videos as well as to your family and friends? Have you ever read any of the heartbreaking accounts of victims of child pornography? Some victims are so young when the abuse starts. Some can't even recite the alphabet yet. Their bodies are so tiny.

I think there's finally been a tectonic shift in my self-esteem. There are hints of self-preservation. And it is about time. After posting on Facebook that I was in Arizona visiting my friend Lili, I got a call from a 602 area code—Phoenix. The number wasn't one of my contacts. Lili's numbers were keyed into my phone. So, unless she was calling from a client's house or another cell phone, it was unlikely her.

"Hello." "Marie . . ." said the booming voice.

"Hey Duane." He'd tracked me down. I won't bother with the backstory of Duane and Marie. Let's just say that Duane is a dead-end street littered with old news and tire marks. I'd rather have a Q-Tip shoved up into my sinus cavities than rekindle that ridiculous, short-lived romance.

"You thought you could sneak into town without calling me." Boom went his deep belly laugh. He loved his sense of humor. The thickly plied playboy insincerity made me cringe. I'd actually fallen for this performance. I politely hurried the conversation along with a bunch of "Yes, yes . . . great, nice to hear from you . . . wonderful." I finally cut him off when he took a breath long enough to squeeze in four words and said, "Well, thanks for calling." This might not seem a huge win to the average person, but for me, it was like winning the Kentucky Derby Trifecta. I now had three wins in my corner. I'd said no to Duane and two other former flames (including Mr. Cum . . . Cum . . . Cum!) by simply ignoring their out-of-the-blue, testing-the-waters emails). For once, no, make that three times, I'd listened to that little voice say, "Yeah, no way. Keep moving forward, Marie."

It has been a decade since I sat Larry down on the sofa and told him we were done. In fact, it's been that long since my last date. I'm not really complaining. I enjoy my alone time. By Friday afternoon, closing out another hectic work week, I'm desperate for *me* time. I don't mind so much when a host asks, "Just one?" I love that it's often easier to find a good, single-seat for a popular movie on opening night rather than convincing a friend to settle for the first row. I enjoy staying up until two or three on Friday nights reading my newspaper and book, doing crafts, and catching up on late-night talk shows without having someone complain about the light and their need for sleep. I have my crafts, dive, friends, work, writing, and books.

But at age fifty-eight, I don't want *never* to have another date. I don't want to forgo another chance at love. Who doesn't enjoy those early relationship butterflies and the *what-ifs*? I don't want never to have sex again with someone other than myself. But, still, I'm scared of being hurt. I don't want to invite trouble into my life. I fear trouble is determinedly lurking around the corner in so many aspects of our lives that I don't want to offer it an open-door policy. When I consider my track record with men, especially my willingness to lower my standards for guys like Larry, I don't trust myself one hundred percent to keep my best interest at heart. My judgment in men, and some friends until now, would average about C+. Some diamonds and some cubic zirconias. But more often than not, I've settled for guys who haven't treated me well.

I lowered my standards for guys who weren't even good place-holders. I've finally reconciled that given the choice of being with someone who's just okay company or being alone, I'd rather be alone. I like my company.

My coworkers and I were trading dating stories and advice. One woman had prepared a list of her perfect man, and at the top was someone who was willing to invest financially in her beauty. And, she said jokingly, guys who didn't make the cut got the "Dear applicant . . . sorry, not sorry" brushoff. One of the women, recently married and far less cynical than Ms. Dear Applicant, told us how she'd met her husband online after months of searching.

"Weren't you scared of all the con artists and wackadoodles," I asked. "How do you really trust that someone isn't a psycho or sicko?" She told us about her own bad experiences and that after the last weirdo, she'd prepared a list of explicit questions and expectations, including no lying. On the first date with any new guy, after all the get-to-know-you calls, texts, emails, and online sleuthing, she'd sit him down on her sofa and interrogate him: previous arrests, pornography habits, sexual preferences, etc. If he refused to answer her questions or was turned off by her interrogation, she'd say goodbye, good riddance. The man who wasn't scared off was the man she ended up marrying. He'd answered her questions and provided her sufficient assurance of his worthiness. She'd done what she could to hopefully avoid reading one day about his arrest for some misdeed. Her story gives me hope.

epilogue
2020

SHORTLY BEFORE THE Coronavirus outbreak caused shut downs around the world, I finished writing this memoir. I felt that Larry and Jane deserved the opportunity to dispute or clarify anything I'd written involving them, so I requested Larry's prison address from Rodney since I'd learned that he continued to support him throughout the years and arrests. I didn't state why I wanted to reach out to Larry. I figured it wasn't Rodney's business to know, but if he asked, I wasn't sure if I'd tell him the truth about the book or simply say I wanted to check in. Rodney replied immediately with a friendly email. He provided Larry's prison address, and added, unsolicited, that Larry was doing well. In fact, he was leading the prison refrigeration and heating repair team. The notion of Larry leading a repair team made me laugh. The prison system must really have a tight budget, I thought. Before I'd had time to thank Rodney for the information, he emailed again the next day to ask if I had written to Larry yet. He shared Larry's email address in case I preferred to reach him that way. It surprised me that prisoners had access to computers, especially those inmates convicted of crimes where computers were an essential tool.

Gathering my courage, I wrote an email to Larry. I said I was offering him the opportunity to dispute anything that I'd written about our thirteen months together. I also asked if he'd ever used my computers to look at child pornography? Was his interest in young children the reason he attended my dive practices and meets? Why did he even date me if he was attracted to young girls? Even though I attached an electronic copy of *Operation Sunflower* (the original title for *Then There Was Larry*), I wasn't sure if it would be delivered. I assumed prisoners' emails were scanned and subjected to review for inappropriate content similarly as letters and packages were. Would words like "child pornography" and "sex" be flagged, causing the email to be returned to me before reaching Larry? Would the staff reply with a stern warning about violating some prison rules? Would Larry find a way to hurt me—emotionally or even physically? Perhaps, but I wouldn't let that stop me. I wanted the catharsis that might come from sharing this book about our relationship and the aftermath. I wanted Larry to read how his lying and crimes affected me and my family as well as so many others. And honestly, I wanted to hurt him by showing him the letter I'd written to Amy Alkon and her response.

I hit send. I figured it was unlikely he would actually reply to my letter or answer my questions. And he hasn't, at least not directly. Simultaneously, I sent a copy of the manuscript to Jane. She, like Larry, deserved the chance to challenge anything I'd written. I also wanted to make her feel bad when she read how betrayed I'd felt.

Within days of emailing Larry, I received an email from Rodney. He was angry that I'd misrepresented my intentions in asking for Larry's contact information. He said he would not have given me Larry's prison address or email had he known my aims. I was asked not to contact Larry again. In closing, he assured me that Larry never used my computer to look at child pornography. I shook my head and wondered to what depths does his loyalty go. His friend was sick and had hurt many of their mutual friends, and yet he stood by Larry. He was definitely a better person than me.

When Jane's reply to my email appeared in my inbox, I froze. I was so nervous that after reading my memoir, she'd say scathing things to me and about me. Maybe there would be threats of a lawsuit. But her email, to my great relief, was compassionate and apologetic. She filled in some gaps and explained that her letter to Larry's attorney, the letter she wrote after initially declining to do so, stated that she believed he was capable of stealthily hiding his sickness and that his sickness was incurable. She asked the judge on behalf of the volleyball family to lock him up for the rest of his life. She told me that everyone who had considered Larry their friend had felt fooled and betrayed. She was sorry that he was in the lives of her children and dozens of others, whom she dearly loved for decades. She told of the long-lasting damage to several relationships, especially with his son after his arrest and sentencing.

Jane and I exchanged emails and then met for dinner. She said she was shocked and saddened at how I'd depicted her and our friendship in the book, but she would accept my perspective. She apologized for the pain and hurt she had caused me and said that she regretted introducing Larry and me in the first place. Regretted that he was ever in my life. Regretted not turning my angry phone call into an opportunity for both of us to process the events and mitigate blame.

"I still don't understand why you introduced us given his past," I said as we sat outside of a seafood restaurant days before the COVID-19 lockdown.

"You were always asking me to set you up. And then, here came Larry, newly single, or almost, and I thought of you. Nothing more premeditated than that."

You were always asking me to set you up. Her failure, once again, to take any responsibility really stung. Suggesting that I had brought Larry into my life didn't seem fair. Granted, I had over the years asked friends and coworkers if they knew of any single men whom they could set me up with. But wasn't that normal? Or had I sounded indiscriminate and desperate?

"You set us up even though you knew he'd been in jail," I said.

"Yes, I thought it was only a few months," she said, adding that she'd truly believed the Home Depot lie he'd told her and their friends. She hadn't known that he had served three years for statutory rape. She described how when he returned to the volleyball group, he went into great detail about the arrest, proclaiming his innocence. He denied any involvement in the whole embezzling scheme. He was simply one of the guys on the loading dock when things went down. He claimed it was a matter of being in the wrong place at the wrong time.

After learning of his arrest for child pornography and speaking with the FBI, she said that she immediately called and/or visited me and all the parents of dozens of children/teens whom she knew Larry had had some contact with on their camping trips over the years. This surprised me, but I also was pleased to know that my instincts about her were not so far off. There was decency and compassion in her. Despite her narcissistic tendencies, but she truly cared about her friends.

"I never knew that Larry had cancer," she said.

"Thyroid cancer, if I remember correctly."

"The bit about living with a foster family was also a surprise."

We mused about whether there were multiple stories that Larry shared with people. Without further research, which neither of us were inclined to do, we would never know what was true and what was false. We agreed he seemed like a guy completely lacking in remorse or empathy—qualities essential to caring about another human being. He was out of our lives, and we could be thankful for that.

Jane and I have kept in contact since this lunch. Our renewed friendship is fragile. We approach it with caution and enjoy the positive aspects of our mutual interests (books, current events, philosophical ideas). I will never deny or downplay the fact that I was hurt, but I know I can forgive—not forget, but forgive and move beyond the betrayal. I can forgive myself, as well, for allowing myself to be hurt and deceived. I can leave behind vestiges of feeling like a victim, and all its negativity, to focus on becoming a stronger woman.

acknowledgements

I am deeply grateful to Sara Marks Brown, Amy Pennington, Lynne Meade, and Derek Douglas for your friendship, feedback, and encouragement. Thank you to Matt Bird for asking the right questions and challenging me to dig deeper. A very special thank you to Angela Dula, copyeditor extraordinaire.

Special gratitude to David Provolo for designing a beautiful book. Much love and appreciation to my talented photographer, Avery Stratford. An immense thank you to Burgess for helping me with the back copy.

Thank you to Corinne, my sons, and friends for helping me to select a title, even though that meant saying no to some of my favorites, including "Boring was the Least of His Problems."

To my sons, I am eternally grateful for your constant love and support. You fill my life with joy and make my heart overflow with love. Thank you for always answering my distress calls for technical support. Much love to my sisters and their families, especially Judy and Scott. Your constant support means the world to me.

To my readers, I appreciate your continued support. I hope you find this cautionary tale useful and engaging.

Marie Estorge is a member of the Squaw Valley Community of Writers. Her debut novel, *In the Middle of Otherwise,* was published in July 2020. She is the author of two previous memoirs, *Storkbites: a Memoir* and *Confessions of a Bi-Polar Mardi Gras Queen*, published under the name Marie Etienne. Her essays have appeared in the *San Francisco Chronicle*, the *Contra Costa Times, Diablo Magazine*, and other publications. Marie and her two sons live in Northern California.